Women Leading School Systems

Uncommon Roads to Fulfillment

C. Cryss Brunner
Margaret Grogan

*A Study Commissioned by the
American Association of School Administrators*

Published in partnership with the
American Association of School Administrators

Rowman & Littlefield Education
Lanham, Maryland • Toronto • Plymouth, UK
2007

Published in partnership with the
American Association of School Administrators

Published in the United States of America
by Rowman & Littlefield Education
A Division of Rowman & Littlefield Publishers, Inc.
A wholly owned subsidiary of The Rowman & Littlefield Publishing Group, Inc.
4501 Forbes Boulevard, Suite 200, Lanham, Maryland 20706
www.rowmaneducation.com

Estover Road
Plymouth PL6 7PY
United Kingdom

British Library Cataloguing in Publication Information Available

Library of Congress Cataloging-in-Publication Data

Brunner, C. Cryss.
   Women leading school systems : uncommon roads to fulfillment / C. Cryss
Brunner, Margaret Grogan.
      p.   cm.
   "Published in partnership with the American Association of School
Administrators."
   Includes bibliographical references.
   ISBN-13: 978-1-57886-282-5 (cloth : alk. paper)
   ISBN-10: 1-57886-282-5 (cloth : alk. paper)
   ISBN-13: 978-1-57886-533-8 (pbk. : alk. paper)
   ISBN-10: 1-57886-533-6 (pbk. : alk. paper)
   1. Women school superintendents—United States.   2. Women school
administrators—United States.   I. Grogan, Margaret, 1952–   II. American
Association of School Administrators.   III. Title.
LB2831.73.B78   2007
371.2′011—dc22   2006021871

∞ ™ The paper used in this publication meets the minimum requirements of
American National Standard for Information Sciences—Permanence of Paper for
Printed Library Materials, ANSI/NISO Z39.48-1992. Manufactured in the United
States of America.

Contents

List of Tables and Figures

LIST OF TABLES

LIST OF FIGURES

Preface

In *Women Leading School Systems: Uncommon Roads to Fulfillment*, Cryss Brunner and Margaret Grogan have provided a fascinating record of the journey women have taken in educational leadership. They have used Robert Frost's poem "The Road Not Taken" as their metaphor for this chronicle of women's journey to the superintendency. They provide the historical context for women who were denied an education, thought to be unworthy of the investment, or educated only so they could serve as their sons' teachers. They explore teaching as the first legitimate public profession for women and note that by 1900, 70% of teachers were women, perhaps due in large measure to their willingness to accept low wages.

Brunner and Grogan state that the superintendency is one of the most heavily masculinized roles in our culture, with women filling only 18% of the superintendencies. They describe the decades-long path that takes women from ranks of uneducated to teacher to administrator. They describe many circular disabling limitations and self-fulfilling prophecies. They analyze the career choices made by women and explore both choices and the superintendency role as a promising career opportunity for women. Clearly and artfully articulated, these authors tell the stories of the road less traveled and the stories of those who took "the one less traveled by."

Extraordinary challenges face our nation and world. Thus, we can't afford to miss or ignore those of ability and promise who can provide much-needed leadership. Our world needs everyone to contribute to his or her fullest measure to making our world better. When talented people are discouraged from pursuing certain career paths, all of society loses out. Brunner and Grogan have provided an important record both of lost opportunity as well as hope for a better tomorrow.

The public school serves 48 million students and 49% of these students are female. *All* of these 48 million children need to see role models who let them know there are no artificial ceilings that limit their abilities to develop and lead. Each child needs affirmations and open doors to success. In order for children to develop as leaders, they must see themselves in the role. They must "see one to be one."

Malcom Gladwell tells the story in the final chapter of *Blink* of the pattern of all-male, all-white orchestras unchallenged for many decades. Change occurred thirty years ago when the judges began to audition the candidates in blind auditions where judges did not see the gender or ethnicity of the auditioner. When the judges began judging purely on the basis of ability, women were selected for orchestras. Gladwell says, "Orchestras now hire better musicians, and better musicians mean better music."

Brunner and Grogan have presented us with a significant challenge that may lead our society to better educators and better educational opportunities. We know the history. We know that a significant segment of the population is not being groomed for leadership. What is our next step?

We all have a responsibility to expand leadership opportunities for those underrepresented in the superintendency. Bravo to those many superintendents who have served as mentors and coaches. The mentoring is a critical step in the process. Bravo to the American Association of School Administrators (AASA) for supporting this research and publication. This professional organization for superintendents is taking positive steps to expand the circle of leaders. Bravo to all those who serve to promote unlimited talent development in all people. And bravo to Brunner and Grogan for highlighting this critically important topic in such an artful and compelling manner.

Maya Angelou in "On the Pulse of Morning" provides the perfect launch pad:

> I, the Rock,
> I, the River,
> I, the Tree,
> I am yours—
> Your passages have been paid.
> Lift up your faces,

You have a piercing need
For this bright morning dawning for you.
History, despite its wrenching pain,
Cannot be unlived, but if faced with courage,
Need not be lived again.
Lift up your eyes upon this day breaking for you.
Give birth again to the dream.

Sarah Jerome, Ed.D
President-elect, AASA
(Second woman president in AASA's 141-year history)
Superintendent, Arlington Heights School District 25
Arlington Heights, Illinois

We dedicate this book to
all women who provided data for this book's birth,
all women who lead school systems,
all women who dare to travel uncommon roads

We wish to thank the American Association of School
Administrators, Joe Schneider, Sharon Adams-Taylor, and
Cynthia Prince for their constant support throughout
the research process.

Margaret also wishes to thank four dedicated, hardworking
graduate assistants at the University of Missouri-Columbia for all
their helpful insights and technical assistance with the project:
Khamthoune Butts, Sheldon Watson, Melissa Griggs,
and Stacey Preis.

Finally, Cryss wishes to thank Yonglyun Kim, graduate assistant,
who worked tirelessly throughout the project, offering helpful
ideas and invaluable technical skills.

Model: Two Roads Diverged in a Yellow Wood

The Road Not Taken

Two roads diverged in a yellow wood,
And sorry I could not travel both
And be one traveler, long I stood
And looked down one as far as I could
To where it bent in the undergrowth;

Then took the other, as just as fair
And having perhaps the better claim,
Because it was grassy and wanted wear;
Though as for that the passing there
Had worn them really about the same.

And both that morning equally lay
In leaves no step had trodden black.
Oh, I kept the first for another day!
Yet knowing how way leads on to way,
I doubted if I should ever come back.

I shall be telling this with a sigh
Somewhere ages and ages hence:
Two roads diverged in a wood, and I—
I took the one less traveled by,
And that has made all the difference.

—Robert Frost (1916, p. 9)

Introduction: The Yellow Wood—
The Terrain of Uncommon Roads

Two roads diverged in a yellow wood. . . .

—Robert Frost, (1916, p. 9)

The "yellow wood" of educational administration is fairly common terrain, yet difficult for women to traverse—think of the undergrowth and hidden obstacles.

While seeking opportunities in the yellow wood, women—who began their journeys by spending time in various administrative positions—come upon "two roads" at some point. When top women administrators are faced with the fork in the road, we imagine their question: "To be or not to be a superintendent?" Indeed, the one less trodden (by women) is the uncommon road of the superintendency, and the other, which is similar in many respects, is the way of the central office administrator who chooses not to go into the superintendency.

Historically, the travelers and uncommon roads about which we write have only recently been chronicled. Some travelers do not think about or may even purposely stay away from the most uncommon road of the superintendency, while others determine to take it. With a deep interest in these journeys—all of which are a bit hidden in the undergrowth—we write this book to describe two types of travelers: those who wish to become superintendents and those who do not.

To explain, we have written a book about women who lead school systems. And while there are some books, chapters, and articles about different positions of school leadership and the women in them, this book is different in several distinct ways. First, this book is grounded in data from not only women superintendents but also from women assistant/associate/deputy superintendents. Women in the central office are rarely the focus of published works. Second, the data used for the book is the largest set ever collected from women assistant/associate/deputy superintendents and superintendents.

Third, because we have gathered data from this group of women, we now have a picture of women (1) in what can be called the normative position to pursue the superintendency and choosing not to; (2) in a position to pursue the superintendency and choosing to pursue it; and (3) in the superintendency. Having these three data sets allows us to compare and contrast the three groups—something that has never been done before. Indeed, since well over half (71%) of our sample of superintendents have served as central office administrators before their superintendencies, we now have a picture of women on the step of the career ladder that is the most commonly taken road to the superintendency. We do note that other roads—those that do not include time in the central office—are taken to the superintendency. And finally, because we have responses from more women of color superintendents and more women of color central office administrators than have been collected before, at long last, we have a richer and more complex picture of their lives and work in educational administration.

The first section's chapter 1, "An Uncommon History," provides a brief historical overview of women and top leadership positions. In other words, we roughly sketch a picture of the terrain in which the yellow wood grows and cast it as a backdrop for our later descriptions of the women who traverse the terrain and come upon the yellow wood. Once the backdrop is established, we begin our portraits. The second chapter, "Aspiration and Uncommon Roads," focuses on the nature of aspiration and how it plays a part in the lives of women candidates.

The second section captures the images of women who occupy top leadership positions as central office administrators. We have chosen to cast these images in two chapters: (1) chapter 3, "Standing at the Fork in the Road," focuses on the *similarities* between women central office administrators who do not aspire to the superintendency and those who do aspire; and (2) chapter 4, "Choosing the Road Less Traveled," focuses on the *differences* between women central office administrators who do not aspire to the superintendency and those who do aspire. Simply, the second section of the book uses our metaphor to provide pictures of women posed in the yellow wood—one group that has no interest in entering the superintendency and another that is determined to enter the role.

The third section is devoted to women superintendents—women who have chosen one of several roads through the yellow wood and are living their lives at the top of public school systems. Chapter 5 profiles women in the superintendency, and chapter 6 profiles women of color in the superintendency and central office. Finally, the book's concluding chapter captures a previously unrecorded occurrence that, in our view, appears to drive women along roadways in the yellow wood and on to aspire into the superintendency—that of *optimal experience* or *Flow* (Csikszentmihaly, 1990).

CONSIDERING THE TERRAIN

CHAPTER 1

An Uncommon History

I shall be telling this with a sigh. . . .

—Robert Frost (1916, p. 9)

Researchers and others who study or pay attention to the history of women and top leadership roles in public education often discuss the topic "with a sigh."[1] The sigh usually accompanies the fact that any general history of the public school superintendency is one primarily about white men. Indeed, in many histories of the superintendency, women are not mentioned at all.

To be sure, research that is focused narrowly on women in the superintendency is a relatively recent phenomenon. The need for research on contemporary women in leadership, broadly speaking, was noted as early as the 1970s,[2] and literature about women in various educational administration roles began to appear in the 1980s.[3] While this particular genre of literature grew, very few empirical studies addressed experiences of women in the superintendency.[4] It wasn't until the 1990s that literature about women in the superintendency proliferated. A group of researchers began to write, think, and publish on the topic.[5]

People often believe that general information about the superintendency applies to anyone—a man, woman, white, or of color—who might be a superintendent. Such a belief holds some truth but lacks an understanding of the fuller story. The fuller story reveals that, since the creation of the position in the early 1800s (Butts & Cremin, 1953), white men have held 82 to 99% of all superintendencies, with the 99% figure occurring in 1980 (Blount, 1998; Brunner, Grogan, & Prince, 2003; Glass, Björk, & Brunner, 2000).

Indeed, while the numbers have always been relatively small, there have been some years in which women have had greater success in accessing the role. For example, during the early 20th century, women seeking school leadership roles were supported by suffrage activism and the women's movement. Support was strong enough that, by 1930, women filled almost 28% of county superintendencies and 11% of all superintendencies (Blount, 1999, p. 9). At the time, Ella Flagg Young, superintendent of Chicago schools from 1909 to 1915, projected that women would soon dominate school leadership in the same way they did teaching (Shakeshaft, 1989, p. 18). In fact, the years 1900–1930 were referred to as the "golden age" for women in school administration (Tyack & Hansot, 1982). In reality, although there were more women in administrative positions during that era, women were found primarily in the less desirable elementary school principalships and in county and state superintendencies. These positions held less stature, rarely served as stepping stones to preferred positions, and paid considerably less than the secondary principalships and district superintendencies (Tyack & Hansot, 1982). During this "golden" period, women made modest gains into the "lower strata of the upper crust" (Connolly, 1919, p. 841, cited in Shakeshaft, 1989, p. 34).

Following the 1940s, women exited the field of school administration to give over their administration positions to the men returning from war. Many returning men pursued teaching and educational administration with support from the GI Bill—legislation that provided their necessary retraining for a smoother reentry into society. Preceding military conflicts, some men chose the education profession as a means of avoiding the draft because these were protected positions (Blount, 1998). This discriminatory practice, based on sex and favoring the entry of men over women into administrative positions, continued into the 1960s and beyond.

Historically, attention to discrimination by sex accompanied attention to discrimination by color during the Civil Rights Movement. The passage of the Civil Rights Act in 1964 and Title VII, both of which addressed women's employment rights, allowed women the opportunity to file grievances for sex-based job discrimination. Due to loopholes in the legislation and a reluctance of the Equal Employment Opportunities Commission (EEOC) to enforce compliance, acts of discrimination continued. In 1972, Congress added Title IX to the Civil Rights Act and provided even greater coverage against sex-based discrimination by providing language that leveled financial penalties on institutions in noncompliance. Federal funding could be withheld from institutions found to be in violation of Title IX.

The Women's Educational Equity Act of 1974 followed Title IX. Federal funds were designated for the purposes of researching and correcting sex-based inequalities in the nation's education system (Grogan, 1999; Shakeshaft, 1989). In spite of landmark legislation to equalize opportunity, women's representation in the superintendency has significantly lagged behind that of men.

Certainly, even when published, figures on the numbers of women in superintendencies have often been misleading because most data reported have been based on the numbers and percentages of women in what Blount (1998) described as the local superintendency. In fact, while Shakeshaft (1989) and Montenegro (1993) reported the percentage of women in the superintendency in 1970 as roughly 2%, they were referring only to superintendents of local districts. Blount (1998), who went further and reported the percentages and numbers of women in *all* types of superintendencies (p. 180), supported Shakeshaft's and Montenegro's conclusions when she noted that, from 1910 to 1950, women held between 9 and 11% of the total positions. She continued by noting that a severe decline occurred after 1950 and, by 1970, women filled only 3% of all superintendencies. Currently, a full 95 years after Ella Flagg Young's famous proclamation, women still hold only 18% of the highest public school leadership positions (Grogan & Brunner, 2005a).

To be sure, in a story in which white men dominate, white male voices are so strong that sounds from other groups are impossible to hear (Brunner, 2003; Kowalski & Brunner, 2005). This dilemma was highlighted by Tallerico (1999) when she stated, "Of the approximately seventy-five years worth of extant scholarship relevant to the superintendency, most studies have either relied primarily on White, male samples, or have made no mention of the gender, racial, or ethnic backgrounds of their subjects" (p. 29).

Over the past 20 years, the story of top administrative roles in education has broadened to include the voices of women and people of color. The resulting fuller story is important to women and people of color for several reasons (Kowalski & Brunner, 2005, p. 150–151):

- Both groups need appropriate and accessible role models.
- Both groups need to understand that following the masculine leadership models found in literature is not a requirement for success.
- Both groups may find themselves practicing in ways that are not mentioned in general books on the superintendency, but their practices are valid approaches to the work.
- Both groups may experience limited access to the superintendency because criteria for selection processes are based on white male norms.

Our version of uncommon history about how women and persons of color have come to the superintendency falls into five large sections: (1) the first section draws attention to historical patterns that created personal and professional space for women and persons of color in education, broadly speaking; (2) the second section highlights the history of how educational administration opened for more women and persons of color; (3) the third section describes how women moved into the superintendency; (4) the fourth section discusses the effect of feminized and masculinized roles; and (5) the last section poses the possibility that the new requirements of the superintendency may create greater access and opportunity for women and persons of color.

CREATING SPACE IN EDUCATION FOR WOMEN AND PEOPLE OF COLOR

In this large section, we provide a history of how women moved into professional education roles.

A Reluctance to Hire Women

With beginnings in religious training, schooling for white male children was conducted almost exclusively by literate white men. Women, girls, and persons of color of all ages were socialized to respect and rely on white men's authority and wisdom, and to fill social positions that required no education (Kowalski & Brunner, 2005). Covert education of these three groups existed for a few individuals, however. For example, as Jackson (1999) reminded us, "We now know that even during slavery, black women had the courage to defy the law and teach slaves to read. They knew that the very survival of their race depended on education" (p. 147).

Even as "schoolmaster" became a clearly defined role, white men, rather than women or persons of color, constituted the group approved to deliver "for pay" teaching services to families who could afford them (Blount, 1998). Massachusetts passed laws in the mid-17th century requiring parents to educate their children. Other states followed suit. Such increased demands for schooling required more schoolmasters—a post viewed as unattractive or as a temporary position by most qualified white men (Waller, 1932). To be sure, even as communities struggled to hire schoolmasters, they remained reluctant to hire women and persons of color for at least three reasons (Kowalski & Brunner, 2005): (a) white women were commonly thought to be less intelligent than white men, (b) since white women had little or no formal schooling, they were not qualified to teach others (Blount, 1999), and (c) persons of color were not considered at all—histories of their role in and experience of education are scarce to nonexistent into the mid-20th century (Jackson, 1999). When noting historical attitudes toward the education of women, it is surprising that any of them ever became superintendents.

Women Become Teachers

As the need for schoolmasters increased, supporters of formal education for white women—Abigail Adams, for example—began to appear (Blount, 1998). In another example, Catharine Beecher's promotion of white women teachers was particularly effective because she argued that women should dominate the domestic sphere as well as any extension of the home, such as the education of children. Beecher's beliefs that white women made natural teachers were later endorsed by Horace Mann as he worked to eliminate teacher shortages (Blount, 1998; Gribskov, 1980). Going further, Benjamin Rush also

provided generally accepted rhetoric justifying education for [white] females; [white] women should receive education for the benefit of their sons, and by extension, the republic. Consequently, Rush's ideology of

republican motherhood failed to challenge existing gender roles and
relations deeply, perhaps a requirement for its acceptance at the time.
(Blount, 1998, p. 13)

This ideology effectively defended and generated unprecedented
formal seminar, academy, and college education opportunities for
white women from 1790 to 1850 (Blount, 1998). Little is known about
educators of color during this time period, although slaves who had the
good fortune of learning how to read and write certainly passed on that
precious education—often risking their lives in the process.

When a convergence of conditions occurred in which qualified white
men found teaching less than appealing and numbers of primarily
white women were educated for the benefit of their sons, white women
eventually moved into teaching positions. In part, because capable
women teachers and activists like Emma Willard and Catharine Beecher advanced the notion, by the early 19th century, single and married
white women slowly became acceptable sights in public schoolrooms
across the nation (Kowalski & Brunner, 2005). In another sector of life,
persons of color—often women—provided their own schooling when
and where they could outside the lives of whites (Jackson, 1999).

Adding to this the fact that women's lack of work opportunities
made them willing to take low wages, the acceptance and numbers of
women grew until in 1900 they accounted for around 70% of all teachers. After the Civil War, while most teachers were white, "Black men
and women rapidly entered teaching, especially in schools built for
Black children throughout the South. By 1900, as many as 20 percent
of women teachers in the South were Black" (Blount, 1998, p. 37). One
hundred years later, women of all colors still significantly dominate
teaching ranks. Teaching, then, is "feminized [because] women constitute [a large] proportion of the teaching ranks, but also feminized in
the sense that the work . . . fit[s] traditional notions of women's work"
(Blount, 1998, p. 21).

The brief slice of history (Kowalski & Brunner, 2005) recounted in
this section spans the years from the formation of our nation to 1900.
In this recounting, several points were made:

- In the beginning, only literate white men were teachers.
- Women of all ethnicities were thought to be of lower intelligence than white men and therefore were not educated.
- Teaching was a white masculine occupation.
- Demand for teachers increased at the same time white educated men became unavailable.[6]
- Early feminists justified the education of white women with the rationale that women at home should be able to educate their sons. Such work was framed as an extension of women's domestic work.
- Once white men were convinced that white women were the appropriate teachers of their sons, education for white women increased.
- Once white women were educated and white men were less available, some women were hired.
- Because teaching was the first (legitimate) public profession for women, women were willing to accept low wages in order to experience the benefits of financial independence.
- After the Civil War, African Americans moved into teaching jobs primarily in the South.
- By 1900, 70% of teachers were women, 20% being women of color, and the role was considered feminized.
- Feminization of teaching meant that (a) the role was considered primarily women's work, (b) it was a fairly low-status role—making it also open to persons of color in the South, and (c) wages remained relatively low (p. 161).

There are numerous historical elements missing from this simplified story, but these highlights help us catch sight of how the professional role of teaching was opened to women.

WOMEN MOVE INTO ADMINISTRATION

In her book *Destined to Rule the Schools: Women and the Superintendency, 1873–1995,* Jackie Blount (1998) pointed out the fact that while teaching became feminized, administrative roles became masculinized. Along with others, Blount (1998) maintained that it was not coincidental that teachers' independence and decision-making powers were stripped away just as women dominated the profession numerically. The male educators who remained had to assert their masculine qualities somehow, thus many became administrators to control the labors of women just as fathers and husbands long had done in the home. Administrators did not appear in significant numbers until women began filling teaching positions. (p. 27)

While white men have always dominated administrative roles, the fact that women gained access to teaching positions resulted in their eventual move into administrative ranks (Shakeshaft, 1999). White women (activists) teachers slowly convinced individual state governments and state and national organizations (headed by men; Reid, 1982) that they deserved to vote for school officials because they (a) owned property and (b) had the right—along with the men who taught and who could vote—to decide which school officials would determine their working conditions (Blount, 1998; Shakeshaft, 1999). By "1910, twenty-four states had granted women school suffrage" (Blount, 1998, p. 66). Women's suffrage had a powerful effect. As Blount (1998) wrote,

The women's suffrage movement had sparked the emergence of women school administrators for at least two reasons. First, the quest for women's rights had triggered the larger movement of organized women's groups, many of which actively supported the candidacy of women for school offices. Second, suffrage had given women power at the ballot box, which allowed them to affect the political process directly, to become, as some had hoped, a political constituency. (p. 81)

WOMEN MOVE INTO THE SUPERINTENDENCY

In this section, we review the history of how women moved into the superintendency.

Women and the Superintendency

At the beginning of the 20th century, thousands of white women moved into school leadership positions, including the superintendency (Hansot & Tyack, 1981). By 1930, 11% of all superintendents were women—although most had jobs at the county level (Blount, 1998). The distinction that most women had jobs at the *county* level is an important one.

Over the past century, superintendents could be found in a variety of settings. To bring definition to these various types of districts, Blount (1998, p. 180) divided them into three classes: (1) state, (2) intermediate, and (3) local. (Others refer to this category as "unified districts"; see, for example, Bell, 1988, p. 41.) County-level superintendencies—the level in which most women superintendents worked—fall in the "intermediate" classification. Blount described the district classifications as follows:

- *State:* agency designated for supervision of public schools for an entire state or territory
- *Intermediate:* administrative organization between the state education agency and local school district; districts where chief administrators do not directly supervise schools (such as county, intermediate district, parish, district, and division)
- *Local:* administrative unit where the chief administrator provides direct supervision of the schools. (Blount, 1998, p. 180)
- Intermediate superintendencies could be likened to central office positions in current times. And true to history, women still have greater access to central office positions than they do to *local* superintendencies.

When considering all superintendencies, as stated before, by 1930, 11% were women (Blount, 1998). The percentage, however, began to plummet after the end of World War II as the women's movement lost its intensity, and masses of men returned to postwar life and sought work in educational administration (Shakeshaft, 1989). By 1980 the numbers of women in the superintendency had sunk to an unbelievable 1%. Not until the end of the 20th century did the numbers of women superintendents again increase to around 14% of all superintendencies (Brunner, Grogan, & Prince, 2003; Glass, Björk, & Brunner, 2000). Over the course of an entire century, the numbers of women in the superintendency increased only a mere 5%. In no small measure, during the 20th century, the superintendency stubbornly remained a masculine role.

People of Color and the Superintendency

Superintendents of color were practically nonexistent before the U.S. Supreme Court's *Brown v. Board of Education* decision of 1954. Of course, there were notable exceptions. For example, one African American woman, Velma Ashley, served as superintendent in Oklahoma from 1944 to 1956 (Revere, 1986). Three other African American women had assumed superintendencies by the early 1970s (Blount, 1998; Jackson, 1999; Revere, 1986). In addition, a

> black superintendent, Alonzo Crim, was appointed [in Atlanta] in 1972 as a condition of the court order [*Brown v. BOE*], demonstrating the expanding role of the court in school decisions. Little was done, however, to desegregate the Atlanta schools until extensive court litigation forced action in the 1970s. (Jackson, 1995, p. 18)

The numbers increased slightly over the decades following the 1970s. In 1981–1982, about 2.2% of superintendents were persons of color, and by 1998, 5% of all superintendencies were filled by persons of color (Cunningham & Hentges, 1982; Hodgkinson & Montenegro, 1999). Unfortunately, in the earlier years, because the data were not disaggregated by gender, we had no way of knowing how many women of color this represented. This percentage remained the same at the beginning of the 21st century (Glass, Björk, & Brunner, 2000) when we were able to ascertain that of those 5%, 1% were women (see Table 1.1). In no small measure, the current superintendency remains a position filled primarily by white men. The superintendency is one of the most heavily white and masculinized roles in our culture. Our current 2003 study reflects the percentage of women in the superintendency at its historical high of 18 percent.

THE EFFECTS OF FEMINIZED AND MASCULINIZED ROLES

Clearly, while the current culture of teaching is feminized, throughout history the culture of educational administration—in particular, the

Table 1.1.   Ethnicity by Gender of Representative Sample

| Race | Gender (% of Total Sample) | | | |
| | Men (86%) | | Women (14%) | |
	No.	%	No.	%
Black	38	2.0	15	5.1
White	1833	95.3	272	91.5
Hispanic	27	1.4	4	1.3
Native American	15	0.8	2	0.7
Asian	3	0.2	2	0.7
Other	9	0.5	2	0.7
Total	1947	100.0	297	100.0

Source: Glass, Björk, & Brunner, 2000, p. 104.

superintendency—has been and is masculinized. But, so what? Before discussing the importance of these observations, we review what is meant by feminization and masculinization.

We have chosen to use Blount's (1998) definitions to begin our discussion. Blount considered teaching "feminized [because] women constitute [a large] proportion of the teaching ranks, but also feminized in the sense that the work . . . fit[s] traditional notions of women's work" (Blount, 1998, p. 21). We extrapolate from her definition of "feminized" that administration can be considered masculinized because men constitute a large proportion of the administration ranks, and because the work fits traditional notions of men's work.

We highlight at this point that we mean stereotypic notions of the nature of women's and men's work when we echo Blount's use of the terms "traditional notions of work." The stereotypes that accompany teaching and administration have existed over years, and while they may have faded a bit, they still shape these two cultures. Teaching, which was only done by men in the beginning, has been considered the work of instructing and caring for children, while administration has been thought to be taking charge of the school or district. Gendered distinctions between rational and emotional, or between instrumental and expressive, roles have historically been used to justify school-based work segregated by sex (Bell & Chase, 1995). The work touted as the more expressive work of teaching children was delegated to women, while what was considered the instrumental or rational work of managing a school was given to men (Bell & Chase, 1993; Strober & Tyack, 1980; Tyack & Hansot, 1990). In sum, in terms of stereotypic understandings and constructions of the roles, when women *and* men move from teaching into administration, they have traveled from a feminized culture into a masculinized one.

No doubt, the work of teaching is feminized whether it happens in elementary schools or high schools, and the work of administration is masculinized whether it happens in elementary schools or high schools. But, within each category—teaching or administration—there are degrees of feminization or masculinization. To begin, teaching can be divided into categories from "heavily feminized" in elementary schools to "somewhat feminized" in high schools because the highest percentage of women teachers is in elementary schools. In like fashion, building-level administration can be divided into categories from "heavily masculinized" in high school to "somewhat masculinized" in elementary schools. Interestingly, overall, high school administration is more masculinized than district-level central office work. And within central office administration, finance positions are more "heavily masculinized" than are curriculum and instruction positions, with other positions falling in between. But any of these masculinized positions pales when compared to the most heavily masculinized position of all—the superintendency. Consider Grogan's (1996) reflections about the roots of the superintendency:

> There is no doubt that once upon a time the superintendent was conceived of in distinctly male terms. In the 1950s and 1960s for instance, the "modern" superintendent was likened to the new executive in peacetime America. Although not used to describe a superintendent of schools, such epithets as "the Man in the Gray Flannel Suit" or the "Organization Man" characterized the image he presented to the public. (p. 12)

Without a doubt, the superintendency is a masculinized role and, when women move into this role's environment, they have traveled from their earlier, perhaps more comfortable, experiences in the feminized territories of teaching.

THE CURRENT AND FUTURE SUPERINTENDENCY

Upon reviewing the history and current status of women and persons of color in the superintendency, one question comes distinctly to the fore: Are there signs that, as with the teaching profession, the superintendency is a more likely career option for women? Does the history of women teachers (white and of color) provide us with a pattern of how disadvantaged groups move into a profession?

To begin a response, one can point out several similarities between women and teaching and women and the superintendency. First, teaching, in early stages of American history, was dominated by white men, just as the superintendency is currently dominated by white men. Second, at one time, women and persons of color, for various reasons, were thought to be inappropriate candidates for teaching positions. The same is true for the superintendency.

Third, an increased demand for teachers occurred at the same time when white men were finding the role less desirable. In parallel fashion, recently there has been a focused concern about the dearth of superintendency candidates (see, for example, Anthony, Roe, & Young, 2000; Houston, 1998; McAdams, 1997). At the same time, men have reported that the job has less or about the same status than it once did, while women and persons of color have reported that it has a greater amount of status (Glass, Björk, & Brunner, 2000). Women and persons of color have also reported a greater amount of self-fulfillment from the role than have men (Glass, Björk, & Brunner, 2000; Grogan & Brunner, 2005).

Third, advocacy in the form of research and publications for women superintendents and superintendents of color now exist that did not exist as little as 15 years ago. Perhaps the recent, although not large, increases of women and persons of color in the superintendency have been the result of this literature and the need for qualified candidates. Fourth, research has pointed to the existence of feminine attributes (Brunner, 2000a; Grogan, 1996; Helgesen, 1990; Rosener, 1990; Sherman & Repa, 1994; Wesson & Grady, 1995)—such as a predisposition toward collaborative work and a focus on instruction. Fifth, women dominate educational administration programs currently, and persons of color, who were once denied an education, have growing access.

As stated earlier in the chapter, for teaching to become dominated by women, meant that (a) the role was considered primarily women's work, (b) it was a fairly low-status role—making it also open to persons of color in the South, and (c) wages remained relatively low. Consider, then, that (a) if feminine attributes of leadership have become valuable—would this mean that the superintendency is women's work? (b) the status of the superintendency appears to be dropping, and (c) salaries for women (white and of color) superintendents are not much higher than salaries for women central office administrators (Grogan & Brunner, 2005)—does this make women and persons of color more attractive superintendency candidates? These questions have yet to be answered. However, if the qualifications and leadership approaches that are necessary to perform the required work are those often exhibited by women, then in this era of accountability, women may be more attractive superintendency candidates than they have been in the past.

With the history of women and people of color in the superintendency as a backdrop, and the suggestion that the superintendency is possibly becoming a stronger career option for women, the next chapters of the book move into the fuller story of aspiring and nonaspiring women assistant/associate/deputy and seated superintendents.

ENDNOTES

1. This chapter is drawn, in part, from T. J. Kowalski and C. C. Brunner's "The school superintendent: Roles, challenges, and issues" in F. W. English's *The Sage handbook of educational leadership: Advance in theory, research, and practice* (Thousand Oaks: Sage, 2005), pp. 142–67.

2. See, for example, Schmuck (1975) and Sexton (1976).

3. See, for example, Biklen and Brannigan (1980); Edson (1988); Gaertner (1980); Marshall (1985); Ortiz (1982); Ortiz and Marshall (1988); Pitner (1981); Schmuck, Charters, and Carlson (1981); Shakeshaft (1989); Shakeshaft, Gilligan, and Pierce (1984); and Wheatley (1981).

4. See Bell (1988); Frasher, Frasher, and Hardwick (1982); Maienza (1986; Pitner (1981); Wiggins and Coggins (1986); and Young (1984).

5. Among these are Alston (1999); Banks (1995); Beekley (1999); Bell (1988, 1993, 1995, 1996); Blount (1998); Brunner (1997, 1998a, 1998b, 1999a, 1999b, 1999c, 2000a, 2000b, 2002a, 2002b, 2003, and 2005); Brunner

and Schumaker (1998); Chase (1995); Chase and Bell (1990); Glass (1992); Grogan (1996, 1999); Grogan and Henry (1995); Helgesen (1990); Jackson (1999); Kamler and Shakeshaft (1999); Méndez-Morse (1999); Ortiz (1982, 1991, 1999); Ortiz and Marshall (1988); Ortiz and Ortiz (1995); Pavan (1999); Pitner (1981); Rosener (1990); Scherr (1995); Skrla (2000a, 2000b); Skrla and Benestante (1998); Skrla, Reyes, and Scheurich (2000); Sherman and Repa (1994); Tallerico (1999); Tallerico, Burstyn, & Poole (1993); Tallerico and Burstyn (1996); Grady, Ourada-Sieb, & Wesson (1994); and Wesson & Grady (1995).

6. "Several reasons for the decline of male teachers have been advanced by historians and others of the time: a) low wages made the job unattractive to capable men, b) the status of teaching was considered 'belittling' to men because it was poor work (Bardeen, 1908; cited in Blount, 1998), c) arguments that teaching was women's work made it less appealing, d) men did not like working with women, and finally, e) during the Civil War, thousands of men left teaching to fight and not many returned to the role after the war (Blount, 1998)" (Kowalski & Brunner, 2005, p. 161).

CHAPTER 2

Aspiration and Uncommon Roads

Then took the other, as just as fair
And having perhaps the better claim,
Because it was grassy and wanted wear

—Robert Frost (1916, p. 9)

When a woman stands at the fork in the road, she spends time pondering whether to take one or "the other, as just as fair." She may choose the less trodden path of the superintendency—"And having perhaps the better claim, Because it was grassy and wanted wear." We wonder about the women who make this choice and ask, What is different about women who choose the superintendency? What is unique about their attitudes, circumstances, and other characteristics? In other words, what creates the desire to aspire to the less traveled road in the first place?

Deeper questions follow: What is aspiration, and why is it important? Clearly, for some things to happen, someone has to *want* to make them happen; in other words, someone has to aspire or have the will to act. In our story of women leading school systems, we find that even some successful women in top central office administration—women poised to move into the position—do not wish to move; they do *not* aspire to the superintendency.

But why are we interested in the decision to turn away from the less traveled road of the superintendency? In our view, such a decision is of interest for two primary reasons: (1) only a small percentage of superintendencies are filled by women (see chapter 1), and (2) currently, some assert that at the national level there is a dearth of superintendency candidates (Glass & Björk, 2003; Kowalski, 2003; Tallerico, 2003). Given these concerns, let it suffice to say that we need to know not only the profiles of women who do and do not aspire to the superintendency but also need greater understanding of *why* they do or do not aspire (see chapters 3 and 4).

To lay the ground for chapters 3 and 4, this chapter first highlights the current discussion focused on the dearth of superintendency candidates, and then moves into a wider discussion of the meaning and nature of *aspiration* itself and things that may create it. Aspiration as a concept is explored through motivation theory. The chapter ends by outlining several scholars' ideas about how motivation is impacted by gender.

THE DEARTH OF SUPERINTENDENCY CANDIDATES

According to various sources, public education in the United States is facing a leadership crisis. The results of a national survey on the school superintendency indicate that the chief executive officers of the nation's schools are concerned about future recruitment and retention of strong, qualified superintendents. Of those superintendents surveyed, 88% agreed that the shortage of applicants for the superintendent's job is a serious crisis in American education (Cooper, Fusarelli, & Carella, 2000). In addition, 92% are concerned that high superintendency turnover creates a serious problem when we wish to keep strong leaders in the role (Cooper et al., 2000). State legislators and administrative organizations such as the National Association of Elementary School Principals, the National Association of Secondary School Principals, and the Educational Placement Consortium have also reported that there is a "steadily growing shortage of school leaders" (Young & McLeod, 2001, p. 462).

Educational leaders and others interested in education have invested resources to determine strategies and solutions for attracting more interest in the school superintendency, and "ironically, within the discourse surrounding the crisis, little consideration has been given to gender even though there is a disproportionate underutilization of women nationwide in educational administration (Bell & Chase, 1993; Grogan, 1999; Nogay & Beebe, 1997)" (Young & McLeod, 2001, p. 462). To be sure, in the recent past, researchers predicted that, as more women occupied the positions of assistant superintendent or director, more women would ultimately occupy the top position of superintendent (Schmuck, 1982; Scherr, 1995). These predictions have not held. Only a small number of superintendency positions have been filled by women compared to the greater number of women in central office positions. There is no doubt that the largely untapped resource of qualified women candidates is underutilized and, due to numerous factors, it is clear that a number of women do not aspire to the superintendency. To be sure, attention to the phenomenon of career aspiration could lead to the future resolution of this leadership crisis.

MOTIVATION: PREDISPOSITION FOR ASPIRATION

The initial stirrings of conversations about human motivation began over 300 years ago with the assertion that the body and the will are distinct (Descartes, ca. 1650). Once humans began to view actions as falling into two distinct camps—the biological and the psychological—our worldview shifted. We started to view the biological nature of our actions as innate and defense oriented, and to allow that a psychological component to our existence is proactive and socioemotionally oriented. People began to have conversations about when, why, where, and how we have control over our life choices and to discuss human existence in terms of motivation theory or the purposeful movement towards goal achievement. The *American Heritage Dictionary of the English Language*'s (Morris, 1981) specific definition of motive is "emotion, desire, physiological need or similar impulse acting as an enticement to action" (p. 56). Because various theorists approach the concept of motivation differently, definitions vary. For the purposes of this chapter we use Young and McLeod's (2001) definition of career aspiration:

> Career aspiration is understood as a three-dimensional concept made up of a woman's career commitments, positional goals, and leadership orientations. In other words, a woman's aspirations include what she hopes to accomplish during her career in education, the types of positions she is interested in pursuing, the goals she hopes to realize while in such

positions, and the leadership styles she believes she must practice to reach her goals. (p. 469)

Theories of motivation ask why individuals behave the way they do in the domains of interpersonal, social, conscious, and/or unconscious contexts (Cavalier, 2000; Hall, 1961; Stewart, 1982; Weiner, 1985, cited in Mountford, 2001, p. 30). Mountford (2004) summarized the overarching points established in motivation theory: "Motivation theory, from the field of psychology, generally suggests that people are motivated to 'act' in some capacity for personal reasons, altruistic reasons, or some combination of the two (Allport, 1960; Cavalier, 2000; Hall, 1961; McClelland, 1975; Weiner, 1985)" (p. 707).

Generally speaking, then, motivation leads to action. Multiple speculations abound about why people are motivated to act. The literature on motivation theory is extensive, at times contradictory, and beyond the scope of this book. To provide context for understanding the findings of our study, we touch briefly on some of the more relevant components of motivation theory. Necessarily, some aspects of motivation are not highlighted. For example, how motivation is created by biological characteristics and needs—such as instinct, eating, thirst, and reproduction—is not discussed in any detail. Because these and other aspects of motivation theory fall outside the scope of our data, we set them aside in large part.

THE DEVELOPMENT AND NATURE OF MOTIVATION THEORY

In this section, we review the historical development of motivation theory and work to determine which literature is relevant and which is not. We do not go so far as to outline a framework for examining our data. Rather, we construct this chapter, for the reader, as a tool or scaffold for puzzling through the data found in the rest of the book. At times, in upcoming chapters, we offer our thoughts about how the data might be interpreted through the lens of motivation theory, but most often leave such musings to the reader.

The Beginnings of Two Major Approaches

Beginning with early 20th-century work, the two major approaches to motivation theory have been referred to as "regulatory" and "purposive." The regulatory approach is grounded in a biological tradition and can be traced to "Darwin's theory of evolution and to experimental medicine. Complex behaviors were interpreted as 'strings' of reflexes, and so, it was theorized, understanding reflexes could also lead to understanding complex social behaviors" (Beck, 2004, p. 25). This approach focuses on the body's response to internal forces such as hunger and pain and the way the body works to return to equilibrium—homeostasis (Beck, 2004). For the purposes of the book's focus, we set aside regulatory motivation theory.

The second major approach to motivation theory—purposive—is much more relevant for our book because it emphasizes the "goal-directed" nature of behavior. This approach is "future-oriented and relatively less concerned with the physiology of regulation" (Beck, 2004, p. 25). The purposive approach is concerned with *why* a person chooses one goal over another. An early 20th-century theorist, McDougall (1923), who moved toward the purposive approach, described instinct as a combination of (a) our tendency to head toward a specific goal by paying attention to specific options that lead us toward a goal, and (b) the emotional excitement that accompanies increasing proximity to goal achievement. Instinct, then, drives us either toward or away from the goal or object (McDougall, 1923). We may then be motivated to take action based on our past and current experiences.

Modern motivation theorists have worked to bring the two major approaches together to provide a fuller way to discuss motivation. They have had some success by drawing attention to a basic motivational premise—that is, that organisms seek pleasant outcomes and avoid unpleasant ones. Thus, desire and aversion—considered intervening variables—are cast along a continuum (hedonic continuum) running from strong aversion, through neutral, to strong desire (Beck, 2004, p. 26). Beck (2004) provided a list of motivational concepts that fall under "desire"—"need for achievement, positive incentives, rewards, cognitive consistency, love, hope for power, relaxation"—and a list of motivational concepts that fall under "aversion"—"fear of failure, negative incentives, punishers, cognitive dissonance, fear, fear of power, stress" (p. 30). In Maslow's (1970) view, such motives are hierarchical and are prioritized by basic needs. However, there is little supporting evidence for Maslow's hierarchy of motives (Beck, 2004). Thus, in our pursuit of motivation theories that inform our data, we find ourselves sorting and sifting theories that may or may no longer be considered valid; theories that are a mix of regulatory and purposive types; and theories that we hear discussed (even when no longer considered valid—for example, Maslow's hierarchy of needs) and those we think might be useful even when we never hear them mentioned in connection with our topic.

Later Blended or Fuller Motivation Theories

Emotions and Motivation

Because emotions are tied to our feelings of pleasure and displeasure, they have been cast into categories of rewards and punishments that either encourage or discourage behaviors (Rescorla & Solomon, 1967; Rolls, 1999). Early theorists who studied emotion shifted the emphasis from a focus on emotions to one on physiology (Cannon, 1927) because of the effects of emotions or feelings on the body. Thus, emotions have, along with desire and aversion, been defined as intervening variables, with "environmental events as antecedent conditions and verbal reports of experience, behaviors, and physiological changes as consequent conditions" (Beck, 2004).

A complete discussion of emotions is impossible given the limited space, but in short, many theorists find commonality around two large points:

> First, emotion is concerned with reactions to rewards and punishments, learned or unlearned. Motivation involves the control of behavior through the anticipation of such rewards or punishers. Second, there is only a small number of specific emotion systems, perhaps three or four. . . . Without any "standard" theory of emotion, there is no complete integration of motivation and emotion to satisfy everyone. . . . In summary, emotion and motivation are intimately related regardless of

what theoretical approach to emotion we may favor. At a particular time, one approach may be more appropriate, whereas at a different time another approach may serve better. (Beck, 2004, pp. 67–68)

Drive and Activation

With its beginnings in the regulatory approach to motivation, drive theory focuses on the idea that humans must maintain homeostatic balance by behaving in ways that return them to equilibrium. Thus, drive is created from an internal need and results in behaviors that satisfy that need. In fact, Miller (1951) suggested that strong and continuous stimuli energize behaviors or drive. Within drive theory, goals are thought to be factors (e.g., reduction of pain) that reduce the drive that created the behavior. Thus, a person is not active until there is some level of need/drive to energize the activity that reduces the drive or, in other words, energizes activity to reach a goal (Beck, 2004, p. 152).

Drive created by basic needs (hunger, thirst, pain) are often referred to as *primary drives,* a name that distinguishes them from drive that is in part a result of learning or conditioning (Hull, 1943). Learned drives are called *secondary* or *acquired* drives. Of the two types of drive theory, we find secondary drives the most relevant for our study.

Brown (1961) studied learned drive in humans by analyzing the "desire for money," as it relates to anxiety or fear and the reduction of both. Brown suggested that stimuli that accompany the condition of not having money become the stimuli for the arousal of fear and anxiety. This particular fear can result in an adult's need to earn money.

Activation theory, like drive theory, has been used to explain why particular behaviors are energized or carried out. Some theorists who focused on activation theory (Duffy, 1934; Hebb, 1955; Lindsley, 1951; Woodworth & Schlosberg, 1954) were more interested in the physiology of drive. Studies focused narrowly on physiology are not useful for the analysis of survey data gained through self-reports.

Interestingly, however, a few activation theorists found that the psychological response to environments that contain intense physical stimuli such as loud noises and frightening experiences produce high arousal and thus activate or energize behavior (Berlyne, 1960). In contrast to most of the theories discussed earlier, in Berlyne's theory, behavior energized by environmental stimulation and arousal is not driven by homeostatic need. Activities that fall into this category are ones that seek stimuli that have one or more of four characteristics: novelty, uncertainty, conflict, and complexity (Beck, 2004). As Beck (2004) stated, "We thus have approach and avoidance behavior that is 'motivated' by something other than homeostatic imbalance and that is reinforced by something other than restoration of homeostatic balance" (p. 172). Another finding of this research was that different environments produce different levels of arousal and are categorized as either high-load (complex and require high effort to deal with) or as low-load (simple and repetitive) environments (Beck, 2004). In addition, people vary in how much they are aroused by different environments and are categorized as either screeners (people very sensitive to selected parts of their environments and who recover quickly from environmental load) or nonscreeners (people less selective in what they respond to and aroused longer after load is reduced) (Mehrabian, 1979, cited in Beck, 2004, p. 173). Without a doubt, superintendents live in high-load environments, and the way they react to such environments has a great impact on their success and satisfaction in the role.

Rewards and Reinforcers

The law of effect and other theories. One early example of regulatory theory, the law of effect, articulates that, through multiple trials of the same activity, we will either repeat or discontinue a behavior based on whether the consequence of the behavior is pleasurable or causes us discomfort (Thorndike, 1911). According to Thorndike, whose work was based on early or old ideas by the standards of his time, the pleasurable effect of a behavior serves as a reward, and we become driven toward incentive-oriented responses. When there are rewards available, we not only tend to be motivated, but also can distinguish if we want to take or avoid action. Rewards within the context of this theory are considered "'reinforcers' because they 'strengthen' the likelihood that a rewarded behavior will occur again" (Beck, 2004, p. 186). Within Thorndike's law of effect, the focus was on how reinforcement is a strong enough condition that it changes behavior. There was no focus on how reinforcers actually work.

The focus of his work led Thorndike to define learning as the formation of a connection between a stimulus and a response, or the S-R bond, with learning strengthened by the use of reinforcers. In no small measure, Thorndike's work has been set aside because strong evidence points to the fact that "most instrumental learning does not consist of such S-R bonds" (Beck, 2004, p. 180). Clearly, the S-R bond does not explain all learning.

Skinner (1938, 1953) took Thorndike's work further by defining a reinforcer as any stimulus that follows a behavior and that increases the probability that the behavior will occur again. Skinner defined *punishment* as a stimulus that follows a behavior and diminishes the likelihood that the behavior will happen again.

Stimulus theories. In contrast to drive-reduction theorists, Harry Harlow (1953) advanced that learning is not dependent upon drive reduction and that external stimuli are more important sources of motivation than internal drive states (Blum, 2002). He concluded that deprivation quite naturally increases behaviors (like eating) that are already familiar to animals. Through experimental research, Harlow and others (e.g., Bower, McLean, & Meacham, 1966) found that some animals are curious about and explore their environments, and that exploration is in itself a reinforcer of behavior of future exploration or learning.

Intrinsic and extrinsic motivation. Intrinsic motivation is defined as behaviors that are enjoyable and rewarding in themselves. In contrast, extrinsic motivation is created by an outside force or person and not under the control of the person performing the rewarded behaviors. Interestingly, the introduction of external rewards for already interesting tasks may reduce enjoyment of or performance on a task— something called the *overjustification effect* (Lepper & Greene, 1978).

Self-determination theorists (Deci & Ryan, 1985) found that the overjustification effect occurs when a person perceives that his or her control over his or her behavior has been taken over by the reward or person providing the reward, something that results in a loss of autonomy. If the reward is verbal praise, however, feelings of competence tend to be the result for the person producing the behavior and thus, the behavior is slightly increased. Increased competence tends to create stronger intrinsic motivation and enjoyment in both adults and children (Deci, 1975; Lepper & Greene, 1978; Sansone & Harackiewicz, 2000).

Interestingly, Eisenberger and Rhoades (2001) found that external rewards did not eliminate intrinsic motivation or creative activity. In summary, the level of intrinsic motivation in a person is created by three psychological needs: autonomy, competence, and relatedness (connection to other people).

Frustration, Anxiety, and Stress

In this section, we highlight theories about three states of mind or emotion that strongly impact motivation and are therefore important pieces of motivation theory. First, in his experiments with monkeys in 1928, frustration was observed and identified by psychologist Tinkle-paugh. He observed three elements: (1) the monkey expected a certain reward, (2) the monkey was given something less than expected, and (3) the change in the reward created disturbance in the monkey's behavior—something from which an emotional response like frustration is taken (Beck, 2004). As Beck (2004) stated, "Frustration is an important explanatory concept because it involves the reactions to aversive states when there is no prior aversive stimulus. Frustration grows out of positive expectations that are not fulfilled" (p. 250). Frustration, then, is a motivator toward behavior when one's goals are thwarted, but the behaviors evoked are as various as in the case of other motivators. Emotional responses may range from disappointment to anger.

The level of frustration as it relates to goal attainment varies in some of the following ways: (1) A number of frustrations related to the same goal can result—at the last experience of frustration—in what appears to be extreme behavior. In other words, frustrations accumulate. (2) The larger the anticipated goal, the greater the frustration. (3) Frustration varies with a person's perception of goal attainment. If the person believes strongly that the goal is attainable, and it is not attained, frustration is greater. (4) Frustration is greater the more an individual values the goal. (5) The more an individual has invested in reaching a goal, the greater the frustration (Beck, 2004, p. 252). And finally, perhaps most interesting in our discussion of aspiration to the superintendency:

A concept called frustration tolerance is sometimes used to account for the fact that different individuals respond to frustrating circumstances with different degrees of emotional intensity. Some people maintain great equanimity and others become highly emotional. This may in part be due to differences in a stable personality characteristic. . . . For example, if a person has survived many frustrating experiences and learned that "things work out," it is easier to remain calm. (Beck, 2004, p. 253)

Some later theorists found that frustration could actually create drive. That is, Amsel (1992) found that when an animal expected a reward and none was given, it tended to move even faster toward what it imagined was yet to come. In addition, rewards only provided part of the time—partial reinforcement—actually increase the number of times that a behavior will be repeated in anticipation of a goal.

Also of interest, as it relates to our study, is conflict theory (Miller, 1959)—within which conflict is understood as a category of frustration. In some cases, conflict arises when an organism has two somewhat equal goals, and one of them cannot be reached if the other one is pursued. An example can be found in role conflict theory, when women believe that they must choose between motherhood and a career. Miller (1959) and his associates asserted that the closer an organism was to either a positive or negative goal, the tendency to approach or avoid became stronger. We speculate that as women move closer to their goal to become superintendents, their knowledge of the position becomes fuller. Thus, their opinions about the goal become more fixed—that is, their opinions about whether the superintendency is either a positive or negative goal become established. Evidently, according to our data, 40% of women in the central office decide that the superintendency is a positive goal and the remainder decide it to be negative (see chapters 3 and 4).

Second, biological theories of anxiety can be found in the mid-20th century, but later theories of anxiety are more useful when thinking about aspiration. For example, Barlow (2000) posed a general theory of anxiety as it relates to emotions, and a number of scholars (Eysenck, 1997; Williams, Watts, McLeod, & Mathews, 1997) advanced cognitive approaches to anxiety that emphasized environmental factors and the way events are perceived by individual organisms. Gray's (1982) work tends to blend both the cognitive and the biological factors into his theory. His theory casts punishment or nonreward as anxiety producing, with the caveat that an organism's perception of the punishment or nonreward—in terms of just how dangerous or catastrophic either would be—is what creates an organism's level of anxiety. In short, high-anxiety participants interpret events as more threatening than do low-anxiety participants, and tend to remember negative events more often than good events—something that reifies a participant's anxiety level.

Finally, theories about stress define the term in three ways: (1) as specific environmental conditions (danger) that create arousal or *stimulus definition*; (2) as a state characterized by the emotional fight-flight reaction, or *response definition*; and (3) as a stimuli and response reaction during an organism-environment interaction in which the demands on the organism are ones with which he or she cannot cope, or *interactive definition* (Beck, 2004, p. 267). The last definition is the most useful when thinking about stress.

According to stress theorists, there are multiple sources of stress— traumatic events, recent life changes, hassles, environmental load, crowding, and noise (Bell, Fisher, & Loomis, 1978; Cohen & Weinstein, 1981; Holmes & Rahe, 1967; Lazarus, 1981, cited in Beck, 2004). To be sure, opportunities for stress abound in the superintendency. Thus, an understanding of the nature of stress and how people react to it is important for people interested in the role. Not surprisingly, stress research has shown that people react differently to stress. In his work with rats, Levine (1960) found that while common sense might dictate that infant trauma should result in emotional disorders, in fact, either mild shock or a daily need to handle stressful events promoted emotional stability. One might take the grand leap from rats to humans and draw from Levine's findings that a somewhat stressful career could facilitate emotional stability and, at once, a sense of wellbeing.

The concept of control plays a part in stress theory, as the lack of control appears to create negative physiological results such as gastrointestinal ulcers. Humans tend to develop strategies for gaining *perceived control,* so that even when control is not a possibility, stress is reduced (Beck, 2004). Perceived control is not a simple idea because even helplessness may be a type of control (Rothbaum, Weisz, & Snyder, 1982). Rothbaum et al. (1982) asserted that people first try to control events (primary control) and, if such an effort fails, people adjust to the events (secondary control) using several different devices:

- *Predictive control* is achieved even in failure situations; failure becomes a predictable outcome and can be dealt with.
- *Illusory control* is achieved even in chance situations; a person may attribute chance outcomes to personal skill. Even the luck that one might have at throwing dice becomes a type of personal skill.
- *Vicarious control* can be gained by identifying with powerful others. The most intolerable situations, including prison camp, can be tolerable to a person who believes that God is on his or her side.
- *Interpretive control* can be gained if a person can find meaning in uncontrollable events, such as "This is a test of my faith, so I shall accept it." All these variations on control help alleviate the stressfulness of a situation.
- Overall, methods of gaining control are just as variable and idiosyncratic as methods of getting food or of getting rid of pain (Beck, 2004, pp. 272–273).

Another theory related to control was advanced by Heider (1958) and was focused on how people look for reasons for their own behavior or that of other people. Another group of scholars—Abramson, Seligman, and Teasdale (1978)—defined three large dimensions of attribution related to helplessness: (1) internal versus external locus of control—such as when failure at some activity is attributed to oneself or to an external event; (2) stable versus unstable causes—a stable cause lasts, an unstable one varies; and (3) global versus specific—an attribution could apply to a large number of events or to one event. These particular attributions in specific combinations appear to result in depression. In fact, in a study of undergraduate students, Seligman, Abramson, Semmel, and von Bayer (1979) found that depressed individuals attributed negative outcomes to more internal, stable, and global factors than did other students. Later, in additional large-sample studies, these findings were upheld (Coyne & Gotlib, 1983; Hammen, 1985) but causality has not yet been established.

In terms of personality characteristics and their relationship to stress, some researchers have asserted that various traits moderate the effects of stress. For example, Type A behavior patterns—patterns characterized by anger, aggression (Hecker, Chesney, Black, & Frautschi, 1988); hardiness—someone with "low neuroticism" (Funk & Houston, 1987) and/or committed to goals, challenges, and feeling in control of life (Kobasa, 1979); and extraversion—someone open, talkative, adventurous, optimist, and sociable (Taylor, 1989) appear to mitigate stress for people.

Finally, as stated earlier, one of the positive side effects of coping with stress is mental and emotional stabilization. People who regularly cope with stress appear to employ numerous strategies that fall into three categories: changing environments and lifestyle, changing personality and perceptions, and directly modifying biological responses (Beck, 2004, p. 281). Specific stress coping techniques include meditation, biofeedback, and focusing on the problems that create the stress. Without a doubt, coping with stress is an extremely important aspect of a superintendent's life and work.

Personality Theories

Regarding the relationship between personality and motivation, Cavalier (2000) asserted, "Motivations supersede personality—motives do not stem from personality, but a pattern of motives assigns personality" (p. 39). Personality theories include motivational and nonmotivational aspects of human characteristics. For our purposes, however, in this section we focus only on the motivational aspects of some of the most relevant personality theories. The primary question for personality theory is: "What kinds of goals impel particular people to action?" (Beck, 2004, p. 321). As a result, definitions, identifications, and organizers of goals have been important.

Some personality theories (Dollard & Miler, 1941; Lewin, 1935) that are labeled *dynamic* categorize goals into two groups: (1) nomothetic goals—those attributable to groups; and (2) idiographic goals— those attributable to individuals (Beck, 2004). Henry Murray (1938, cited in Beck, 2004) and others cast goals into different categories, *presses* and *needs*. In Murray's division, presses are external states (environmental), and needs are internal states. He then divides needs into two different types: (1) *viscerogenic*—related to body needs and changes, (2) *psychogenic*—not related to body needs. In the latter category, Murray identifies several needs, of which three are often studied—achievement, affiliation, and power.

Achievement Motivation

Two of achievement theory's primary theorists were John Atkinson and David McClelland. Atkinson (1958) pointed out the importance of personality structure for understanding motivation. He believed that motivation is based on a person's hope of success or fear of failure; that is, motivation is highly dependent on the immediate situation and environment (cited in Weiner, 1985). McClelland's (1971) achievement theory, like Murray's (1938) advanced that individuals tend to hold three culturally based needs that determine future behavior—the need for achievement, power, and/or affiliation (Cavalier, 2000). The assertions of Atkinson and McClelland included interpersonal rather than intrapersonal theories of motivation. They believed that motivation was generated by the individual's relationship to his or her social structure and immediate environment.

According to achievement theory, for example, people with high achievement motivation are more persistent in goal striving and tend to select occupations that are neither too easy nor too difficult for them (McClelland, 1985). Business is a likely choice for highly motivated individuals because there are opportunities in that field to take risks, to measure success in terms of profits and costs, to respond to economic and performance feedback, and to be creative (McClelland, 1985). There is no doubt that the superintendency falls into this genre of occupations.

McClelland (1958) did an interesting study focused on *task preference*. The study included children with high and low needs for achievement. McClelland found that in a ring-toss task, high-achievement children tended to stand a medium distance from the peg and low-achievement children tended to stand either near or far from the peg. This research generated interest in the *level of aspiration*. Work in this area found that people tend to change their goals realistically on the basis of their experiences—failure lowers the level of aspiration and success raises it (Lewin, Dembo, Festinger, & Sears, 1944, cited in Beck, 2004). Criticisms of this work abound, however. As Beck (2004) wrote:

> First, there seem to be more dimensions of achievement motivation than just motivation for success and fear of failure. Second, much of the early research with nAch [need for achievement] was restricted to males, raising the question whether men and women are different in achievement motivation. Research with different measure of achievement motivation than the TAT [Thematic Apperception Test] measures generally shows no sex differences, however. Third, many studies did not find differences between high and low nAch people. (p. 331)

Attribution Theory

Grounded in criticisms of achievement theory—those noting that not all people respond to failure and success in the same way—attribution theory, in particular, takes into account that people may view the causes for success and failure differently. In brief, attribution theory focuses on "1) how and why people search for the causes of their own behavior or that of other people, 2) the kinds of causes that are found, and 3) the effects of such attributions on emotion, motivation, and subsequent behaviors" (Beck, 2004, p. 331).

One theorist, Bernard Weiner (1985), developed categories of possible causes for a person's response to success and failure. One category identifies internal and external attributions—that is, one person may believe that success and failure are strictly her own responsibility while another person may believe that external forces create both (for example, good or bad luck). A second category identifies stable versus unstable attributions—that is, a person may identify his ability (a stable attribute) as a cause while another may believe that the cause is attributable to his effort (an unstable attribute). Finally, another category identifies controllable and uncontrollable attributions—that is, one person may believe that she could have controlled the attribute that caused the success or failure or in another case the same person may believe that she could not have controlled the cause (for example, illness) (Beck, 2004, p. 332–333).

While attribution theory appears to have some value for predicting future achievement behaviors, unfortunately evidence of that possibility is lacking. Thus, while the attribution of a cause could be identified, predictions from such attributions were not reliable (McClelland, 1985). In short, this particular theory is not useful as a predictor of future achievement behavior, and thus, does not help us in our search for why women do or do not seek the superintendency.

Power Motivation Theory

McClelland's (1975, 1985) work spans achievement and attribution theory. Within achievement theory, McClelland distinguished between *personal power* (characterized by dominance over others) and *social power* (characterized as aiming to benefit others). Personal power tends to relate to aggression and competition, and "men high in need for personal power have been found to do more fighting, drinking, gambling, and speeding than men low in need for personal power" (McClelland, 1985, cited in Beck, 2004, p. 337). Interestingly, possibly because of socialization, these characteristics were *not* found in women.

McClelland (1971) and Cavalier (2000) both cast power as an integral part of understanding human motivation. They suggested that individuals are often motivated to act solely to achieve or experience power (Cavalier, 2000; McClelland, 1971). And once power is acquired, it is expressed differently dependent on motive (Cavalier, 2000; McClelland, 1971). For example, a person who is motivated to act for altruistic reasons (social power), and who has acquired power, might believe his or her acquired power offers an opportunity to be generative and to "exert influence upon the world and the environment, and the care of future generations" (Cavalier, 2000, p. 110). Conversely, a person motivated to act for personal reasons and who has acquired power might believe his or her acquired power offers an opportunity to dominate and oppress others to fulfill personal needs, desires, or agendas (Cavalier, 2000; McClelland, 1971). For example, people high in need for power may collect symbols of power such as prestige possessions, like cars and jewelry. People with a high need for power were most interested in teaching, psychology, ministry, business, and international diplomacy, and those with low need were most interested in government and politics, medicine, law, creative arts, and architecture (Beck, 2004).

Job Motivation Theories

Job motivation theories focus on the idea that some aspects of a job allow people to satisfy "higher level" needs, which Frederick Herzberg (1966) called satisfiers or motivators. He suggested that people want more from their jobs than pay, such as responsibility, recognition, stimulation, feelings of achievement, and challenge.

Levels of Motivation

Several ideas in this category were advanced for consideration by Abraham Maslow in 1943. Maslow's (1970) oft-quoted "Hierarchy of Needs" asserts that individuals have levels of basic needs that are fulfilled, beginning with the most fundamental levels and moving through increasingly complex ones. These basic needs are focused on psychology, safety, belongingness, love, esteem, and self-actualization. As each level of need is fulfilled within us, humans necessarily move on to gratify the next level of need. According to this theory, our motivation to act is based on a striving towards the pinnacle of the hierarchy (Maslow, 1970). Motivation, it appears, is generated by a need that people have to develop positive self-regard. Resting on Maslow's theory, Rogers (1942) concluded that human beings are motivated, at the most basic level, toward constructive behaviors that they perceive will lead them to greater self-actualization. The theory, however, is difficult to test because in lower-level jobs, there may be very little opportunity for self-expression (Beck, 2004).

Intrinsic or Extrinsic Motivation

Other researchers believe that two levels of motivation are enough "to account for work motivation. One level combines physiological, safety, and belonging needs, and the other level combines esteem, achievement, and actualization. To be clear, the location, or source, of motivation has been termed as being either intrinsic or extrinsic. Motivation is intrinsic when satisfaction and interest in repeating and completing a behavior is generated from within the individual. Motivation is extrinsic when rewards are outside of the individual such as prizes or awards (Staw, 1976). Intrinsic motivation strengthens an individual's desire to be responsible and to make productive choices. Extrinsic rewards do not encourage prosocial behaviors nor strengthen inner resources (Dreikurs, 1969). An example of intrinsic motivation is "social interest," which is a need to be a part of and a contributing member of the community (Adler, 1917). Motivation may also be self-interest based. For instance, each player in a school—administrator, teacher, student, and parent—is motivated to reach his or her education-related goals. All stakeholders may be motivated to build respect and personal regard within the context of the school as well as to demonstrate competence integrity as they do their work (Byrk & Schneider, 2002).

Job Satisfaction

Job satisfaction is another aspect of job motivation theory. Several job dimensions have been identified (McCormick & Ilgen, 1980; Smith, 1977) and related to job satisfaction. Job dimensions identified were work itself, pay, promotions, recognition, working conditions, benefits, self-supervision, coworkers, customers, and family members. In addition, research testing Lawler and Porter's (1967) model of job satisfaction found that there is "greater job satisfaction when rewards are specifically related to job performance. This finding suggests that job satisfaction comes with perceived control over events that produce success" (Beck, 2004, p. 407).

Job Characteristics

Job characteristics have also been shown to create job satisfaction (Hackman & Lawler, 1971; Hackman & Oldman, 1976; Reith, 1988). Six specific job characteristics were found to correlate with satisfaction: (1) variety of work on the job; (2) autonomy in doing work and making decisions; (3) task identity—doing clearly defined work; (4)

receiving performance feedback; (5) dealing with other people: and (6) friendship opportunities on the job.

Learning

Motivation to perform on the job is also about learning. Rats respond to environmental stimuli that train them to work to either repeat or avoid a consequence based on their behavior. Positive reinforcement occurs when the behavior results in a positive outcome (Skinner, 1938). From the model of operant conditioning, behavior modification programs function when people are given praise and rewards for positive behavior so that the positive behaviors increase in strength and frequency (Hall, Lund, & Jackson, 1968). Research conducted by Harry Harlow (Blum, 2002) and his students, which occurred around the same time as Skinner's, established that learning was an unique activity in that it was its own motivator. To be clear, once engaged in learning, primates were motivated to learn more, even without rewards.

The phenomenon that an activity could be its own motivator (learning, for example) was echoed more recently in Csikzentmihalyi's (1990) work. Csikzentmihalyi (1990) fleshed out other more specific reasons for being motivated to act. In part, he enumerated that we are, at once, motivated to engage and motivated by engagement in (a) activities that are enjoyable, (b) challenging tasks that have clear goals, and (c) activities that have immediate feedback. In brief, motivation and activities that motivate us are inextricably linked if action along a certain path is to continue. Some activities, like learning, are "autotelic," in that they are naturally motivating and enjoyable (Csikzentmihalyi, 1990; see also chapter 7 of this book).

Without a doubt, a look at aspiration through motivation theory draws attention to the complexity of this phenomenon. In our study of women superintendents and central office administrators, we have some findings that reveal tendencies that are informed by this literature set. The rest of this book highlights these and other findings and, in the final chapter, we move deeper into what we believe is the most viable explanation for a person's interest in and aspiration to these top administrative roles.

In the next section, we provide examples of what theorists and researchers have thought about the relationship between gender and motivation.

A FULLER RENDERING OF ASPIRATION: MOTIVATION AND GENDER

To be sure, in a book about women who do or do not aspire to the superintendency, we must add the element of gender to our discussion of aspiration and motivation. In no small measure, sexism is part of the reason that there are so few women in the superintendency (see, for example: Brunner, 2000a; Chase & Bell, 1990; Johnsrud, 1991; Shakeshaft, 1989, 1999; Tallerico & Burnstyn, 1996). Limiting the discussion of why women do or do not aspire to whether women in themselves are motivated is a mistake. Without a doubt, women as a group and individually are affected by sexism in ways that could diminish or even eradicate motivation to aspire. As Tallerico and Blount (2004) noted:

> Numerous scholars have elaborated factors contributing to the persistence of male overrepresentation in educational administration (e.g., Estler, 1975; Montenegro, 1993: Ortiz, 1982; Ortiz & Marshall, 1988; Sadker, Sadker, & Klein, 1991; Schmuck, 1980; Shakeshaft, 1989, 1999). These factors include ideologies about appropriate sex roles, social stereotypes about who looks and acts like a leader, the socialization of children consistent with such stereotypes and norms, the bureaucratization of schooling that was built on separate spheres for women (teaching) and men (leadership), the conceptualization of schooling and its leadership in ways that emphasize competition and authority (stereotypically masculine strengths) rather than collaboration and service, administrative employment practices that present higher barriers for women than for men, and the greater proportion of men than women earning graduate degrees in educational administration up until the mid-1980s. (pp. 641–642)

Overcoming barriers of the type itemized above is difficult and at times impossible for women. Once in administrative positions that have been defined and institutionalized as men's work, such barriers become pointedly overt to most who experience them—a phenomenon reported by numerous researchers (e.g., Blount, 1998; Beekley, 1999; Bell, 1995; Brunner, 2000a, 2000b; Chase, 1995; Chase & Bell, 1990; Grogan, 1999; Grogan & Henry, 1995; Kamler & Shakeshaft, 1999; Rose, 1969; Skrla, 1999; Skrla, Reyes, & Scheurich, 2000; Tallerico 2000a, 2000b; Tallerico & Blount, 2004; Tallerico, Burstyn, & Poole, 1993; Tyack & Hansot, 1982). Reason dictates that women who have aspired long enough to move into central office administration could easily lose their drive to push further toward a superintendency. Thus, while we believe it important to answer the previously stated questions about aspiration, we temper our discussion with a few examples from the literature of how gender can influence and shape women's motivations toward leadership in education. In the next sections, we highlight several examples of theories that link gender and aspiration.

Gender, Age, and Aspiration

In Grogan's (1999) study, many of her participants talked about age and its effect on their aspirations. Most identified that when they could finally consider the superintendency—at the end of family responsibilities—they were also close to the end of their careers. Interestingly, most participants resisted discouragement and continued to hold on to their aspirations regardless of age. Marshall (1985) noted that

> The age norms associated with career steps conflict with women's roles. Males have made crucial career moves in their late twenties and early thirties, building a career norm. For women to go through this male model of entry would require sacrifices of important women's roles or tremendous role overload and conflict. (p. 133)

The study that is the focus of this book brings new information about age and aspiration (see chapter 4).

Gender and the Denial of Aspiration

Marshall (1985) asserted that women who "deny their aspirations and deny that they endure role strain and subtle discrimination, they accede to the normative controls of the school organization, and they retain culturally defined roles" (p. 139). She continued by adding that women who deny role strain and discrimination are able to avoid a "spoiled identity in society and in their careers" and the stigma attached to it, but that such denial results in the end of career mobility (p. 139). Such women typically play the role as teachers and at times elementary principals or other specialist staff positions. Indeed, in our study, a number of the women in our sample had elementary teaching and administration positions.

Internal Barriers to Aspiration

Role Conflict

As discussion in the previous section on the denial of aspiration, when faced with the experience of spoiled identity, women are cast into role conflict (Merton, 1959; Parsons, 1949) in ways that are more profound than a conflict related to making a choice between one role and the other. Indeed, just the basic choice between the roles of wife-mother and career woman can create great anxiety given the time that both take. But when faced with the issue of the stigma attached to the role of career, Darley (1976) asserted that women often avoid the career or achievement-oriented role and accept the mother-wife role (Jones & Montenegro, 1983).

In our study, we found that women in top leadership roles were having children at approximately the same rate as women in the broader population. Clearly, they are not giving up the mother role to a great extent. In some fashion, however, careers in education—with its focus on the care of children—may ease the stigma that accompanies the career or achievement-oriented role of school leadership. Indeed, when examining the literature to see what types of role conflicts resulted when individual needs clashed with normative standards or institutional expectations, Truett (1979, cited in Jones & Montenegro, 1983) found that though role conflict existed for women educational administrators, they were not hindered by it—"they were neither less efficient nor less effective than men"(Jones & Montenegro, 1983, p. 231).

Gender-Specific Attitudes

Some have asserted that women's personal qualities create internal barriers to aspiration. Hennig and Jardim (1977), for example, provided several gender-specific attitudinal barriers: (1) lack of aggressiveness; waiting to be chosen, discovered, invited, persuaded, or asked to accept a promotion; (2) reluctance to take risks; and (3) lack of self-confidence. This literature set tends to blame the women themselves for their lack of aspiration. The results of this book's study, to some extent, set these barriers aside.

External Barriers to Aspiration

In this section we provide examples of society's attitudes, systems, and structures that create external barriers to women's aspiration. This book, in several places, discusses these particular barriers and the extent to which women believe that they inhibit aspiration.

Lack of Sponsorship and Role Models

Several researchers (Gardiner, Enomoto, & Grogan, 2000; Marshall, 1985) have discussed sponsorship and role models. Marshall (1985) discussed sponsorship:

> The most powerful training and mobility structure in the educational administration career, the sponsor-protégé relationship, occurs when a powerful person notices, tests, trains, and promotes a protégé. The sponsor-protégé relationship is a close and personal one. Male sponsors are reluctant to invest their efforts in women because women are different and because close male/female relationships most often are seen as nonprofessional. (p. 133)

Family Responsibilities

While life at home has changed to some degree, women still shoulder the majority of family and household responsibilities. Given the time demands of top administrative roles, women may not aspire to the top because they simply have no desire to take on more responsibility or work. Every woman has different circumstances that influence her capacity to do more. Societal norms do not work in her favor, so she must address this particular aspect of her life in some way in order to move forward in her career.

Perceptions of Female Characteristics

Because educational administrative roles have been most often filled by men, a male model of leadership has evolved. Further, "Women administrators, because of their abilities, different jobs and life experience, special training and interests, may exhibit a leadership style that differs from the expectations for male-normed educational administration positions" (Marshall, 1985, p. 133). Women typically have more classroom experience, and many have it at the elementary level. These experiences, as well as their career paths, formal and informal training, age, and other issues related to gender can create the impression that women lack what is seen as the proper leadership style—that is, they do not exhibit the familiar and accepted masculine persona. Marshall continues:

> Aspiring women, having no power to challenge or change the requirements, must find ways to convince the men in power positions that their ascribed handicaps are unimportant develop *impressions management* [our emphasis] repertoires. Because this impressions management requires time, energy and constant vigilance, it constitutes a barrier to women's entry and mobility in the career. (pp. 133–134)

Stigma and Resentment from Others

The notion of "stigma" (from Goffman's *Stigma: Notes on the Management of Spoiled Identity,* cited in Marshall, 1985) was used by Marshall (1985) to indicate the signs that "disabled, deviant, or deficient people carry" (p. 130). Marshall found that when women administrators were unable to retain the "normal woman or administrator" status and experienced stigma or spoiled identity, they used at least one of three techniques to handle it: (1) denial and retreat; acceptance of cultural and organizational norms related to gender specific behavior; (2)

alienation, rebellion; remaining the "marginal man," and (3) coping with stigma through the use of impressions and situation management; disidentifying, covering, and passing (p. 132).

CONCLUSION

Motivation theories—whether connected directly to gender or not—run broad and deep. Upon reviewing a portion of this extensive literature, one begins to understand why the concept of aspiration is so elusive. We believe that literature on motivation is helpful in understanding aspiration but not the complete picture. Grogan (1996) used Mac-Leod's (1987) definition of aspiration in her book on women aspiring to the superintendency. She stated:

> MacLeod (1987) defines aspirations as "one's preferences relatively unsullied by anticipated constraints" (p. 60). In other words, I have taken aspiration to mean the *hopes of a superintendency* [our emphasis] as the desired occupational outcome of the academic and experiential preparation that motivates certain administrators in the public school systems. Although I heard their fears too, I concentrated on their hopes. Therefore, I looked for women who desired the superintendency for reasons of personal and professional interest. I inquired after the participants whose background and training provided good preparation for the job and whose work in educational administration made them viable candidates in the minds of their colleagues. (pp. 5–6)

We draw on the quote above to establish a fuller articulation of our task. To begin, it is clear that Grogan recognized a connection between motivation and aspiration. She also included several of the components of motivation that have been noted in the literature on motivation. For example, she pointed to past experiences, background, training, and learning. In addition, she connected "desire for the superintendency to reasons of personal and professional interest." In other words, we assert that the tie between motivation and aspiration is a tight and close one. It is not a stretch to state that people are motivated to aspire.

In terms of our sample, we argue that central office administrators create a pool of viable candidates for the superintendency, and a pool that one would assume to be motivated to aspire to the superintendency. Indeed, their positions virtually at the top of school systems indicate that colleagues have supported them over and over again. They have experienced tremendous success. The remaining chapters of the book profile the women in our study in ways that help unpack, to some degree, the various circumstances facing women who do or do not aspire to travel the final uncommon road to the superintendency.

CONSIDERING THE TOP

CHAPTER 3

Standing at the Fork in the Road

Two roads diverged in a yellow wood,
And sorry I could not travel both
And be one traveler, long I stood
And looked down one as far as I could
To where it bent in the undergrowth;

—Robert Frost (1916, p. 9)

As women assistant/associate/deputy superintendents approach the fork in the road, they stand—"long I stood"—and consider their options, that is, whether to move down the road of the superintendency or on down the other road and remain in their central office positions. The larger group of our sample of women assistant/associate/deputy superintendents (60% of them) indicated that they *did not* want to be superintendents. They had decided that they would remain in their central office roles—roles that we recognize as the last step usually taken before moving into the superintendency.

To be sure, these women were and are clearly successful in their careers, for they fill top leadership positions. Of the 472 central office respondents, 18% described themselves as deputy superintendent, 2% described themselves as chief academic officers, and the rest were assistant/associate superintendent for human resources, finance, curriculum and instruction, operations, administration, or support services. We assume that they are talented and skilled, as their roles require both. In short, the fact that they do not aspire to the superintendency is *not* an indicator of failure or lack of talent, ambition, devotion, or skill. Not surprisingly, however, we asked ourselves: Why do women in the pipeline for superintendency positions say "no" to the opportunity?

But first, we have a more pressing question: "What do these women have in common with those who do aspire? Certainly, they cannot differ *significantly* from women who want to be superintendents. In this chapter, we identify the commonly held characteristics of women in the study who *do not* aspire and those who *do*. We caution readers to remember that these general characteristics are those of the greatest percentage of the sample. Therefore, when one thinks about an individual, this general description may not hold. Indeed, individuals in the sample vary greatly.

COMMONLY HELD CHARACTERISTICS OF ASPIRING AND NONASPIRING ASSISTANT/ASSOCIATE/DEPUTY SUPERINTENDENTS

To begin, a few things can be assumed about the entire sample of assistant/associate/deputy superintendents in our study. All are women for whom career is important; they have moved up the career ladder by choice. They could have remained in positions of teaching or building-level administration and directorships/supervisors rather than moving into the upper echelons of the central office. Broadly cast, their desire for advancement cannot be questioned. In addition, the women in our study like their jobs. In fact, 71% of central office administrators indicate that they experience "considerable" self-fulfillment from their work. Therefore, we can assume that these women have been rewarded for their "desire to advance" to one of the highest rungs on the career ladder.

But there are other characteristics and demographics that large groups of these women have in common, and those descriptors are the focus of this chapter. First, we highlight the personal demographics of the largest percentage of the women central office administrators in the study (see Figure 3.1). Second, the demographics of the most common district descriptions are sketched (see Figure 3.2). Third, we identify the professional development opportunities and the types of support from others that they have experienced (see Figure 3.3). Next, we focus on "Getting the Central Office Administrator Job" (see Figure 3.4). The chapter then turns to "Life as a Central Office Administrator" (see

Figure 3.5) and finally follows with "Working with the School Board" (see Figure 3.6).

MOST COMMON PERSONAL DEMOGRAPHICS

The largest percentage of women assistant/associate/deputy superintendents in the study are white (90.5%) and in positions titled associate or assistant superintendent of "something" (about 80%) with 49% of the entire sample being in charge of curriculum and instruction. Over half are Democrats (55%) with moderate political views (62%) and, at the time they responded to the survey, were between 51 and 55 years of age (44%), had lived in either a small town or a suburb before college (66%), completed an undergraduate major in education (57%), and later finished their formal education with an EdD or PhD (49%) in educational administration and supervision (79%), were married (74%), raised or were raising one to two children (57%), and began their education careers as elementary teachers (58%). After spending 6 to 15 years as elementary teachers (58%), between the ages of 31 to 40 (53%), these women took their first administrative positions either in elementary principalships (40%) or as directors/coordinators (34%). By and large, the women's career paths took them from teacher to principal and on to central office administration (48%).

Later, between the ages of 36 and 50 (66%), when hired into the first central office administrative positions, their one to two children were anywhere between six years old and early adulthood. There is no doubt that these women (75%) had raised or were raising children when they first became assistant/associate/deputy superintendents. Around 25% of the women had or have no children. In fact, both aspiring and nonaspiring women agree at about the same rate (34%) that lack of mobility of family members is one of three "important" factors (on which they agree) that limits administrative opportunities. Interestingly, the women also agree at the same rate (about 14%) that lack of mobility is *not* a barrier ("somewhat important" was also a choice option). In other words, the aspiring and nonaspiring assistant/associate/deputy superintendents as an aggregate group split at about 50-50 between those who fell at the extremes "important and not a factor" and those who thought "lack of mobility" was "somewhat important.

- Associate/assistant superintendent of curriculum & instruction
- White, married, moderate Democrat (51–55 years of age)
- 1 to 2 children
- From small town or suburb (before college)
- Undergrad major: Education
- 1st job in education: Elementary teacher (6–15 years)
- 1st administration job (age, 31–40): Principal or director
- 1st hired for central office: 36–50 years old
- Ages of children raised or raising as central office: 0–15 yrs
- Career path: Teacher, principal, central office
- Are not currently seeking a superintendency
- Report considerable job satisfaction
- Most common salaries: $75,000–$125, 000
- Believe hired for: Ability to be instructional leader

Figure 3.1. *Most Common Personal Demographics: Women Central Office Administrators at Time of Survey*

DESCRIPTION OF CURRENT DISTRICTS

At the time of the study, the women assistant/associate/deputy superintendents were most often in either suburban (44%) or suburban/rural districts (an additional 22%) with student populations of from between 1,000 to 24,999 (82%). Of these women, 65% were in districts that had enrollment growth (over the years 1990 to 2003) from between under 5% to 25% or more. Their districts were primarily in three geographic regions (60% of sample): Mid-East, Southeast, and Great Lakes. The great majority (83%) was working in districts with men superintendents, and 85% had *not* been in the same district for their entire careers.

Interestingly, district size had no impact on whether the women chose to aspire to the superintendency. Around 40% of women, regardless of district size category, aspire to the superintendency.

PROFESSIONAL DEVELOPMENT AND SUPPORT

Generally speaking, women central office administrators are extensively educated in formal academic settings. Over half completed an undergraduate major in education (57%) and about half (49%) have either an EdD or PhD in educational administration and supervision

- District location: Suburban or suburban/rural
- District enrollment: 1,000 to 24,999
- District grew between 1990 and 2003
- Geographic region: Mid-East, South-East, Great Lakes
- Residence: Have *not* stayed in one district over entire career
- Never worked with woman superintendent
- In districts headed by men superintendents

Figure 3.2. *Most Common School District Demographics—Women Central Office Administrators at Time of Survey*

(79%), a degree that 63% completed 6 to 15 years ago. About 50% of the women rate their graduate studies as "good" when the choices are "poor, fair, good, or excellent."

The women assistant/associate/deputy superintendents in the study are also professionally educated, as 68% of them have superintendency certification. Additional nonuniversity-based professional develop-ment—which 80% rate almost equally as "useful" or "very useful"—was provided most often by the Association for Supervision and Curriculum Development (ASCD) (77%), the American Association of School Administrators (AASA) (60%), and other state education agen-cies (58%).

Most of the women hold memberships in professional organizations. Those organizations most frequently joined include: ASCD (74%); AASA (57%); and Phi Delta Kappa (41%). Approximately 35% have attended AASA's National Conference on Education, and around 12% attend AASA's Women Administrators Conference. Those who do not belong to AASA (26%), the national organization for superintendents, report that they *do not* for five main reasons: (1) seems to be a profes-sional organization primarily for superintendents, not central office administrators (16%); (2) cost of membership is too high (13%); (3) do not know enough about the organization (12%); (4) have not been contacted to join AASA (11%), and (5) needs are better met by other national associations (10%).

Other opportunities for professional development occur at a more individual level. For example, most of the women in the study read professional journals. *Educational Leadership* is the most frequently read (76%), followed by *Education Week* (63%), *Kappan* (52%), *The School Administrator* (45%), and *American School Board Journal* (37%).

The women in the study agreed that certain issues should be included in preservice and in-service professional development. The issues most often identified as ones that should be included in both pre-service and in-service education are: (1) changing priorities in curriculum (78%); (2) demands for new ways of teaching or operating the educational program (81%); (3) assessing educational outcomes (83%); (4) high-stakes, state-mandated accountability testing (85%); and (5) effective public relations skills (73%).

Other education or professional development comes in different forms. Mentoring, for example, can make a significant difference in whether a woman feels prepared to become a superintendent. In fact, 84% of the women assistant/associate/deputy superintendents themselves had served in the role of mentor for someone else aspiring to be an administrator. Therefore, they understood the importance of mentoring. They participated in mentoring others and knew that they needed it themselves.

GETTING THE CENTRAL OFFICE ADMINISTRATOR JOB

Most of the women assistant/associate/deputy superintendents (76%) in the study believed that the "old girl/boy network" is part of their

---

- Mentor others aspiring to administration
- Mentored by: Both men and women
- Were supported to become central office administrators by men super-intendents
- Undergraduate major: Education
- Highest degree: EdD or PhD
- Major field of study in highest degree: Educational administration and supervision
- Greatest source of continuing professional development: ASCD
- Belong to ASCD and AASA
- Most hold superintendency certificate
- Most read professional journals

Figure 3.3.   *Most Common Professional Development and Support—Women Central Office Administrators at Time of Survey*

work world, and that it helps individuals get central office positions. Along with this network, other groups, such as school boards and search firms, are a part of the search for a new job.

Given the low numbers of women in top educational administration jobs and the political nature of the job search, most women understand that there are barriers to their access opportunities, especially to the superintendency. And while the majority (90%) of the assistant/associate/deputy superintendents were not, at the time of the survey, applying for a superintendency, both aspiring and nonaspiring women indicated at about the same rate that three barriers in particular were important for women wanting a superintendency: (1) 34% identified the barrier of "lack of mobility" of family members; (2) 29% agreed that there was a perception that women are not politically astute; and (3) 25% agreed that there was a perception that instructional and curricular orientations or emphases limit administrative and managerial interest and skills.

The women in the study also were in agreement that some of the barriers listed were "not important" or "not a factor." All the assistant/associate/deputy superintendents identified that the following barriers were "not a factor" and *did not* limit opportunities for women who wanted to be superintendents: (1) interestingly, lack of mobility of family members (14%); (2) lack of opportunities to gain key experiences prior to seeking the superintendency (33%); (3) lack of professional networks (29%); and (4) lack of mentors/mentoring in school districts (29%).

The women assistant/associate/deputy superintendents in the study—those who aspired and those who did not—were in agreement about which knowledge or skills might help advance career opportunities for women superintendents or women aspiring to the superintendency. The two groups, whether aspiring or not, chose each knowledge/skill with the same frequency. The percentages of women who indicated the degree to which particular knowledge might help career advancement follow in order: (1) interpersonal skills (87%); (2) responsiveness to parents and community groups (83%); (3) ability to maintain organizational relationships (82%); (4) emphasis placed on improving instruction (61%); (5) knowledge of instructional process (teaching and learning) (59%); and (6) knowledge of curriculum (57%). In no small measure, the first three are believed to be very important. The next three are also viewed as important by around 60% of both groups. Interestingly, when asked the same question, the women superintendents ordered them in same way and with approximately the same degree of importance.

One other question was asked about barriers to getting the job: To what extent are discriminatory hiring and promotional practices a problem in limiting administrative career opportunities for individuals of color? When answering this question, 43% of aspiring and nonaspiring women agreed that discriminatory practices were a "minor problem" for people of color.

LIFE AS A CENTRAL OFFICE ADMINISTRATOR

When hired at a salary that for 70% falls in a range between $75,000 and $125,000 (with 10% receiving a bonus; 78% of the time the bonus is $5,000 or less), women in the central office appear to have an equal chance to be given a 1-, 2-, or 3-year contract. Around half of the women believe that the most important reason they were employed was their ability to be an instructional leader. This response is predictable, since around half of them were hired as assistant or associate superintendents of curriculum and instruction. Two other reasons for employment are noted at about the same rate (about 23%): personal characteristics (honesty, tact, and others) and potential to be a change agent.

- Believe old girl/boy network helps individuals secure jobs
- Not currently applying for a superintendency
- Most hold superintendency certificate
- Most read professional journals
- 30% agree on three important career barriers
- Around 85% agree on knowledge/skills that are important for career advancement:
    1. Interpersonal skills
    2. Responsive to community
    3. Organizational relationship skills

Figure 3.4.   *Getting the Central Office Job—Women Central Office Administrators Respond to Survey*

Once in their positions, over half of the women in the study perceived that they were "very successful" in their overall effectiveness as central office administrators. However, they did report three main factors that they believed inhibited their effectiveness: (1) too many insignificant demands; (2) too much added responsibility; and (3) inadequate financing of schools.

Of the 95% of the women in the study who were evaluated, 76% were evaluated annually on their job performance through a formal process (40%) or a blend of formal and informal processes (39%). Most (92%) of the women had a formal job description, and half of them were closely evaluated against the criteria in the description.

Both aspiring and nonaspiring women were in close agreement about the purpose of the evaluation process. The three top reasons for board evaluations according to the women in the study were: (1) to document general dissatisfaction with performance (98%); (2) to determine salary for the following year (92%); and (3) to point out strengths and identify areas needing improvement (90%). Finally, 81% of the women indicate that in their most recent evaluation their boards or supervisors had rated them as "excellent."

WORKING WITH THE SCHOOL BOARD

Half of the women assistant/associate/deputy superintendents in the study indicated that they work for seven-member school boards that usually have one woman and no people of color serving on them. Most

---

- Salary: $75,000–$125,000
- Contract: 1, 2, or 3 years
- Hired as assistant or associate superintendent of curriculum and instruction
- Hired for instructional leadership ability
- Rate themselves: Very successful
- Have a formal job description
- Formally evaluated annually
- Board rating of performance: Excellent

Figure 3.5. *Life as a Central Office Administrator—Women Central Office Administrators Respond to Survey*

of the women's board members' terms of service are from 2 to 4 years. Half of the study participants believe them to be "qualified" and actively but not rigidly aligned with community interests. The women believe that the most difficult problem that their board members face is one of finances.

In terms of the work they do with schools board, the assistant/associate/deputy superintendents in the study report that they either develop (35%) or share in the development of policy (33%), and they also report that the board accepts their policy recommendations 90 to 100% of the time. Finally, they voice the opinion that their input for decision making is given more weight by superintendents than by boards. At the same time, they believe that their input is less important to superintendents than the input of principals.

Related to other decision making, they are split about the effects of school-based decision making (SBDM). In fact, 41% believe that SBDM has increased parent and/or community member participation in decision making, and 44% believe that SBDM has made no difference. Over half of the women reported that their school boards were supportive of SBDM, and that as central office administrators, they (57%) frequently seek citizen participation in district decision making.

Clearly, women in the central office, regardless of whether they aspire or not, have many characteristics in common. In the next chapter, we unpack some of the ways that these two groups are different.

- Have seven-member school boards, with usually one woman and no people of color
- Board members' tenure—2–4 years
- Serve as professional advisors to board
- Report that they develop policy (35%) or share in policy development (33%)
- Believe their boards are qualified and not rigid
- Formally evaluated annually
- Board rating of performance: Excellent
- Believe boards accept their policy recommendations 90 to 100% of the time

Figure 3.6.   *Working with the School Board—Women Central Office Administrators Respond to Survey*

Choosing the Road Less Traveled

> Then took the other, as just as fair
> And having perhaps the better claim,
> Because it was grassy and wanted wear. . . .

—Robert Frost (1916, p. 9)

As women stall at the fork in the road to consider their options, around 40% of them choose the road to the superintendency "because it was grassy and wanted wear." That is, they decide that the superintendency looks at least as attractive as various other central office roles and even has added allure. They might ask themselves, "Why not give the super-intendency a try?" And, upon further thinking, the decision is made, "I *will* be a superintendent!"

Thus, on one hand, 60% of women in the yellow wood and on the road to the superintendency say "no" to the opportunity, while on the other hand, the rest say "yes" to the idea. We, however, are still left with the question: Why do some women in the pipeline for superinten-dency positions say "yes" and some say "no" to the opportunity? We began the work toward an answer in chapter 3 by pointing out that the two groups have much in common. Efforts to answer the same question continue in chapter 4, with the highlighting of ways the two groups are different from each other. In order to carry out this purpose, the chapter begins with discussions of the most significant differences between the two groups of women. At times, the data on the women superintendents in the study are used to illustrate how the assistant/associate/deputy superintendents compare and contrast with them. After all, an under-standing of women who have successfully entered the superintendency is necessary before identifying what characterizes viable aspiration to the position. The full picture of the women superintendents can be found in chapter 5.

Chapter 4's first section focuses on significant differences in the aspiring and nonaspiring women's views of barriers limiting advancement opportunities to the superintendency. Next, we offer thoughts about how age affects aspiration.

SIGNIFICANT DIFFERENCES BETWEEN ASPIRANTS AND NONASPIRANTS

This section includes discussions of some of the more significant differences between aspiring and nonaspiring assistant/associate/deputy superintendents in our study. To begin, the two groups' views of barriers to the superintendency are examined.

Two Views of Career Barriers

One item of the study's survey listed a number of commonly identified barriers to the superintendency. Respondents to the survey were asked to indicate whether each listed barrier was an "important factor," "somewhat important factor," "not a factor," or "don't know." When looking at the percentages of aspirants, nonaspirants, and seated superintendents who had indicated that the barriers were an "important factor," we were surprised. Common sense predicted that persons significantly impacted by barriers to a goal—in this case, a position—would be less likely to pursue the goal. What we found flies in the face of common sense.

One surprising difference between aspirants and nonaspirants is the fact that, generally speaking, larger percentages of aspirants over nonaspirants reported that barriers were "important factors" (see Figure 4.1). Apparently in the mind of aspirants, accessing the superintendency is quite difficult. And while some nonaspirants also indicated that barriers to the position are important factors, percentages of them were most often lower than the percentages of aspirants. We were struck when we realized that, when contrasted with aspirants, nonaspirants just did not believe the barriers to be as important. One reason might be that nonaspirants have not considered the position very deeply and thus are not aware of what can be perceived as barriers.

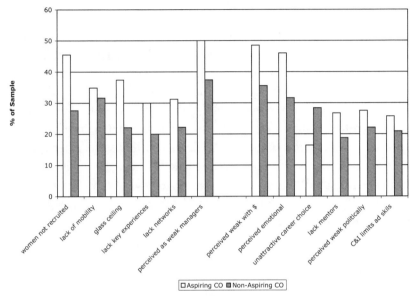

Figure 4.1. *Important Barriers to Superintendency*

In Figure 4.1, one can see that "lack of mobility" and "unattractive career choice" is the only barrier checked "important factor" less often by aspirants than by nonaspirants. This fact may indicate that aspiring women believe that the superintendency is an attractive career choice and have decided that they are willing to move to gain the position.

Four of the barriers were indicated as "important factors" by at least 40 to 50% of the aspirants (in order): (1) women perceived as weak managers by school board members (50%); (2) women perceived as unqualified to handle budgeting and finances (48.5%); (3) women perceived to allow emotions to influence administrative decisions (46%); and (4) women not recruited by school boards (45.5%). Greatest differences (more than 10%) between aspirants and nonaspirants are found in responses to the following barriers: (1) women not recruited by school boards; (2) women experience midmanagement career "glass ceiling"; (3) women perceived as weak managers by school board members; (4) women perceived as unqualified to handle budgeting and finances; and (5) women perceived to allow emotions to influence administrative decisions.

We speculate that when aspirants believe strongly in the existence of important barriers to the superintendency, they pay attention to them in ways that nonaspirants do not. Knowing the barriers (whether perceived or real) to any goal can enable one to address or to be prepared for them. Further, on one hand, challenges can be motivators for many people. Perhaps, when women believe that the road to the superintendency is difficult, they are more motivated to seek it. On the other hand, as achievement theory suggests (McClelland, 1985; see chapter 2), perhaps women who seek the superintendency believe that while barriers to the position exist, overcoming the barriers will be neither too easy nor too difficult for them—in other words, such challenges are just right for these risk-takers.

Thoughts about Age and Aspiration

In this section we explore the relationship between age and aspiration. The exploration is a broad one because age impacts various aspects of life that in turn can affect aspiration. We begin with a section that describes various aspects of age and position and then turn to a topic central to age—that is, motherhood and aspiration.

Age and Position

To begin, we provide the ages of the whole sample at the time of the survey disaggregated by aspiration and position (see Figure 4.2). The purpose of providing the ages of the women superintendents is to illustrate (1) the difference in the aspiring women's ages and the superintendents' ages, and (2) the difference in the nonaspiring women's ages and the superintendents' ages. It goes without saying that women who are not superintendents and who also aspire to the superintendency could be expected, on average, to be younger than women who are already in the superintendency.

In a closer look, Figure 4.3 reveals that aspiring women, indeed, are younger than both superintendents and nonaspiring women. (Data on superintendents is included for these comparisons.) Greater percentages (18%) of aspiring women are under 45 when contrasted with superintendents (7.4%) and nonaspiring women (7.1%). At the other

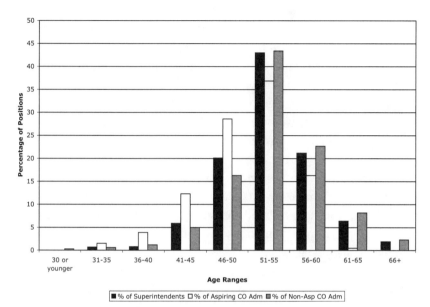

Figure 4.2.   *Position and Age*

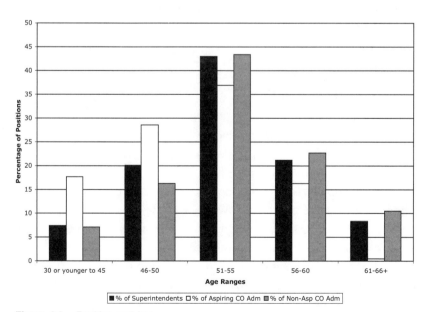

Figure 4.3.   *Position and Age*

end of the range from 61 years of age and older, only a half percent (0.5%) of aspiring women fall into the range, while over 8% (8.3%) of superintendents and almost 11% of nonaspiring women fall into this range. Clearly, nonaspiring women's percentages in all age ranges closely echo the percentages of seated women superintendents.

Given these facts, we note that, in general, age appears to make a difference in whether a woman aspires or not. However, because in almost all age ranges there are groups of women who *do* aspire, we *cannot* say that a woman's age indicates that she will *not* aspire except in the case of women over 60. Evidently, by the time they are 60, women who aspire are already in superintendency positions or they have given up on their aspirations and fall into the nonaspiring group.

What is also clear when considering these percentages is that the aspiring women are younger than the seated superintendents, a fact that supports their desires to seek the role. The earlier that aspiring women become assistant/associate/deputy superintendents, the greater their opportunities to become superintendents. This finding is neither new nor surprising.

What is new, however, is that women's aspirations for the position of superintendent occur early and do not disappear until after 60 years of age. Also surprising is just how young these assistant/associate/deputy superintendents are. Many women are poised on the most common road—positions in central office (CO)—to enter the superintendency at relatively early ages. The common perception that women wait too long to enter the administrative pipeline can, at least in part, be set aside for 40% of our sample.

To further expand an understanding of age and position, Figure 4.4 illustrates the ages at which the women in the study were first hired into an administrative position. There is little doubt that most often (87.6%), women who enter the superintendency have had some type of prior administrative experience, whether at the building level, district level, or both. To be sure, a high percentage of women who want to be superintendents will have or will need administrative experience of some type. Adding this information to the fact that women who aspire are in general younger than those who do not aspire, the age at which women become administrators is significant.

Figure 4.4 displays two things: (1) women who aspire were first

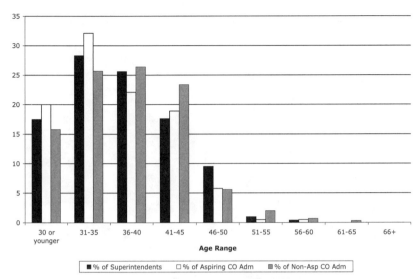

Figure 4.4. *Age at First Administrative Position: Superintendents, Aspirants, and Nonaspirants*

hired as administrators at a somewhat younger age than women who do not aspire, and (2) women who aspire in 2003 are somewhat younger when they first became administrators than the age at which the women superintendents in the study became superintendents. This fact may be an indicator that more women are ready to move into the superintendency at younger ages. When women enter the superintendency at an earlier age, other facts about women in the superintendency have potential to change. For one, once in the superintendency, the length of women superintendents' collective tenures could lengthen. In addition, the fact that aspiring women are younger in the pipeline increases the chances that they will successfully reach their stated goal to become superintendents.

Upon knowing the ages at which the women in the study first became administrators, the ages at the time they first became central office administrators is of interest (the most frequent next step after a principalship—for 54% of aspiring women and 40.4% of nonaspiring women). Figure 4.5 reveals that, again, the aspiring women are just a bit younger than those who do not aspire. Overall, Figure 4.5 looks a great deal like Figure 4.4 with the exception that, of course, the women

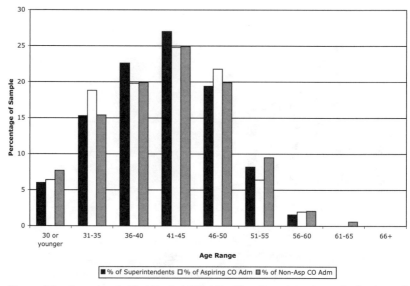

Figure 4.5. *Age when in First Central Office Position: Superintendents, Aspirants, and Nonaspirants*

are all older. Indeed, the highest percentages of women were from 31 to 35 years of age when they first became administrators and 41 to 45 years of age when they first became central office administrators. This fact provides some evidence that women move from building-level administration into district-level administration in around 10 years. Thus, the move from principalship to the superintendency most likely takes *at least* 10 to 12 years.

Other pieces of information about age and aspiration add to a larger picture. For example, Figure 4.6 compares and contrasts the ages (at the time of the survey) of *all* aspirants and nonaspirants with the ages of the aspiring and nonaspiring assistant/associate/deputy superintendents of curriculum and instruction (CI)—who make up almost half of our sample. This comparison allows us to see whether the largest subset of our sample is identical to the larger sample. Not surprisingly, the subset largely echoes the whole sample. Some slight differences between the ages of 46 to 55 and over 60 exist.

Apparently, at the time of the study, the assistant/associate/deputy superintendents of CI were slightly older than the entire sample. In

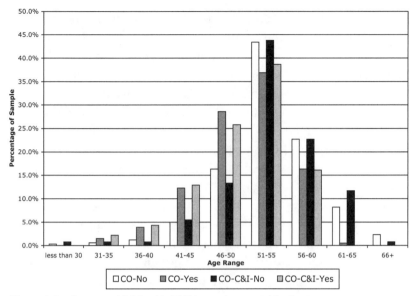

Figure 4.6. Compare All CO with C&I/Nonaspirants and Aspirants

addition, after age 60, aspiring assistant/associate/deputy superintendents of CI disappear, while in the larger sample there are a few women
who still aspire to the superintendency.

Why is this information important? In an era when the role of superintendents has been expanded to include a strong focus on curriculum
and instruction, assistant/associate/deputy superintendents of CI
become a natural pool of likely candidates for future superintendencies.
This subset of women is also the largest group of aspirants and worthy
of our attention. If women who aspire understand that age plays a part
in their career plans, information relative to their specific positions
could make a difference for them.

Age, Motherhood, and Aspiration

Over many years, for obvious reasons, the idea that family obliga-
tions impede career advancements for women has flourished. Indeed,
one belief afoot was that women did not become superintendents
because they chose to raise their children before pursuing the time-con-

suming positions in the central office. Further, after waiting for child-rearing to subside, women were not young enough to gather the experience necessary or were not considered viable candidates because they were too old. Contrary to this popular belief, in chapter 2, we noted that both nonaspirants and aspirants are most often raising or have raised two children. In fact, in terms of the percentages of U.S. women who have no children, there is little difference between the women in our study (18.4% of aspirants; 26.5% of nonaspirants; 23.8% of superintendents) and the general public (19%) (U.S. Census Bureau, 2000).

In this section, we draw attention to a contrast between the two groups; that is, aspirants and seated superintendents appear to be raising more children overall than nonaspirants. Even more interesting, as seen in Figure 4.8, there are fewer aspirants with *no* children than either of the other two groups—nonaspirants and superintendents. This piece of information flies in the face of the notion that women choose between motherhood and the superintendency or that women who aspire put off seeking the superintendency so they can raise their chil-

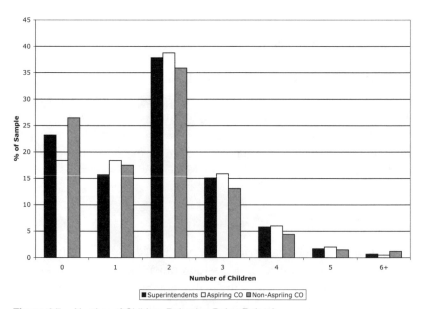

Figure 4.7. *Number of Children Raised or Being Raised*

dren. Also brought into question is the assumption that women who are career focused and driven to advance are less interested in having children than are other seemingly less ambitious women. Indeed, it appears that motherhood is a larger part of the lives of both aspirants and seated superintendents than it is for nonaspirants. As illustrated in Figure 4.8, aspiring women make up the largest percentages of women who are raising children between zero and 15 years of age.

EDUCATION

The discussion in this section is divided into two topics: (1) "Formal Academic Education" and (2) "Professional Education." The subsection "Professional Education" contains two foci: "Professional Organizations and Associations" and "Mentoring and Role Models."

Formal Academic Education

Education matters—in particular, for women. Indeed, previous studies have found that a greater percentage (56.8) of women superinten-

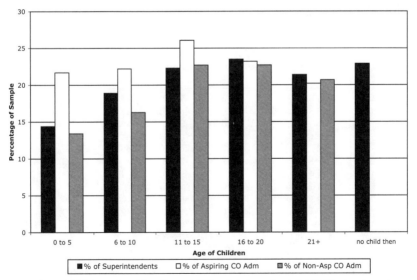

4.8. *Age of Children when First Central Office Admin.—Supt. & CO (Aspirants and Nonaspirants)*

dents than men (44.7) hold doctoral degrees (Glass, Björk, & Brunner, 2000, p. 80). But does education play a part in one's aspiration to the superintendency? Do women with more advanced degrees aspire more often than those with less advanced degrees? Again in this section, to gain greater understanding the characteristics of aspiring and nonaspiring women in the central office relative to the superintendency, data from superintendents are used as well as data from assistant/associate/deputy superintendents.

To begin, Table 4.1 establishes that many women assistant/associate/deputy superintendents and superintendents in this study hold either an EdD or a PhD degree; in fact, 57.7% of female superintendents and 42.8% of assistant/associate/deputy superintendents hold a doctoral degree. More female central office administrators (31.4%) hold an MA in education than do female superintendents (23.7%). When considering district size and the academic degree of female school administrators, there is a difference of frequency between MA holders and EdD or PhD holders. While not surprising, the most interesting fact is that while there is a tendency to find a higher percentage of doctoral degree

Table 4.1. Highest Academic Degree of Women Assistant/Associate/Deputy Superintendents and Superintendents

		District Size				
	Academic Degree	*less than 1,000*	*1,000– 3,000*	*3,000– 10,000*	*more than 10,000*	*Total*
Central office administrators	BA/BS	2(5.7)	0(0.0)	4(1.9)	2(1.0)	8(1.4)
	MA in education	14(40.0)	44(36.1)	58(28.0)	63(30.6)	179(31.4)
	MBA	0(0.0)	2(1.6)	3(1.4)	1(0.5)	6(1.1)
	Specialist	5(14.3)	27(22.1)	33(15.9)	22(10.7)	87(15.3)
	EdD/PhD	8(22.9)	37(30.3)	94(45.4)	105(51.0)	244(42.8)
	Other	6(17.1)	12(9.8)	15(7.2)	13(6.3)	46(8.1)
	Total	35(100)	122(100)	207(100)	206(100)	570(100)
Superintendents	BA/BS	0(0.0)	1(0.5)	0(0.0)	0(0.0)	1(0.1)
	MA in education	80(34.9)	45(22.4)	35(17.9)	11(11.6)	171(23.7)
	MBA	1(0.4)	1(0.5)	1(0.5)	0(0.0)	3(0.4)
	Specialist	44(19.2)	27(13.4)	22(11.2)	9(9.5)	102(14.1)
	EdD/PhD	92(40.2)	117(58.2)	134(68.4)	73(76.8)	416(57.7)
	Other	12(5.2)	10(5.0)	4(2.0)	2(2.1)	28(3.9)
	Total	229(100)	201(100)	196(100)	95(100)	721(100)

Note: x^2 (central office administrators): 34.130 **, df: 15, x^2 (superintendents): 57.263 ****, df: 15. The value of x^2 is obtained from Pearson Chi-Square statistic. ** $p<.01$, *** $p<.001$. The figures in parentheses indicate the percentage of that cell number.

holders than MA degree holders in the large districts, in the small districts the percentage of MA degree holders is higher in the cases of both assistant/associate/deputy superintendents and superintendents.

Against the backdrop provided by Table 4.1, aspiring and nonaspiring assistant/associate/deputy superintendents are next compared to each other. Table 4.2 presents the relationship between two survey questions, "What is the highest degree you hold?" and "Do you aspire to the superintendency?" and the findings are disaggregated by district size. First, survey respondents who aspire to the superintendency have

Table 4.2. (Q041) Highest Degree You Hold by District Size. (Q105) If not currently a superintendent, do you aspire to the superintendency?

Q105			Less than 1,000	1,000– 3,000	3,000– 10,000	More than 10,000	Total
					District Size		
YES	Q041-HIGHEST DEGREE	MA IN ED	3	15	19	11	48
			37.5%	32.6%	23.5%	16.4%	23.8%
		SPECIALIST	2	3	12	13	30
			25.0%	6.5%	14.8%	19.4%	14.9%
		EDD/PHD	3	24	48	39	114
			37.5%	52.2%	59.3%	58.2%	56.4%
		OTHER	0	4	2	4	10
			.0%	8.7%	2.5%	6.0%	5.0%
	Total		8	46	81	67	202
			100.0%	100.0%	100.0%	100.0%	100.0%
NO	Q041-HIGHEST DEGREE	BA/BS	2	0	4	2	8
			11.8%	.0%	3.1%	1.7%	2.4%
		MA IN ED	6	26	43	45	120
			35.3%	38.8%	33.1%	37.8%	36.0%
		MBA	0	1	3	1	5
			.0%	1.5%	2.3%	.8%	1.5%
		SPECIALIST	1	22	20	8	51
			5.9%	32.8%	15.4%	6.7%	15.3%
		EDD/PHD	6	10	47	56	119
			35.3%	14.9%	36.2%	47.1%	35.7%
		OTHER	2	8	13	7	30
			11.8%	11.9%	10.0%	5.9%	9.0%
	Total		17	67	130	119	333
			100.0%	100.0%	100.0%	100.0%	100.0%

Among the respondents to say "yes" to Q105, EDD/PhD holders is the largest (56.4%); among the respondents who say "no," MA holders is the largest (36%).

The number of EDD/PhD holders increases and the number of MA holders decreases as the district size increases. This is a same result to the relationship between "Highest academic degree" and "District size (without Q105)"

the largest percentage (56.4) of EdD and PhD degrees. Second, survey respondents who do *not* aspire have the largest percentage (36) of MAs. The percentage of aspiring women (56.4%) who have an EdD or PhD is essentially the same as the percentage of seated superintendents (57.6%) who have acquired doctoral degrees and is significantly different from the percentage of nonaspiring women (36.7%) with an EdD or PhD degree. These findings suggest that education plays a part in whether women aspire to the top position. Indeed, as motivation theory suggests and as some research has shown (see chapter 2), learning is motivation for additional learning. In no small measure, a move into a position that is unlike any other definitely requires substantive new learning. These findings leave us with numerous questions: If learning motivates one to learn more, or if learning itself is its own motivation, could there be a connection between learning and aspiration to new situations that require new learning? But, which comes first—learning or aspiration? Or are they inextricably linked?

When looking at district size and aspiration, we find that, as in Table 4.1, aspiring and nonaspiring EdD and PhD holders increase and MA holders decrease as district size increases.

One aspect of academic education is the use of educational research to guide one's work practices. In short, if a person experiences more education, that extra education should show up in his or her work life. But, do aspiring and nonaspiring women actually use their educations in their daily work lives? One way to answer this question is to ask women their opinions about the usefulness of educational research. When this question was posed, 56.4% of the aspiring women indicated that educational research is "Highly Useful," while 44.9% of the nonaspiring women thought it "Highly Useful." Thus, whether it was that the education level was higher for the aspiring women (56.4% have doctorates, over the 36.7% of nonaspiring with doctorates) or whether they thought educational research useful regardless of education level, the conclusion remains the same: A higher percentage of aspiring women than nonaspiring women believe educational research to be "Highly Useful."

Professional Education

Education and development comes in many forms. For administrators, professional organizations provide training and development education as well as opportunities for networking with other administrators. Another type of professional development comes in direct relationships with mentors and role models. In this section, both are discussed to answer the question: Do professional education experiences differ for aspiring and nonaspiring assistant/associate/deputy superintendents? First, a subsection compares and contrasts the professional organizations to which aspiring and nonaspiring women belong. A second subsection compares and contrasts the experiences of aspiring and nonaspiring women with mentors and role models.

Professional Organizations and Associations

Administrators belong to myriad organizations and associations for at least two reasons: (1) training and development opportunities, and (2) networking and professional connection efforts. Common sense dictates that people interested in career advancement would necessarily belong to professional organizations and associations. But, do aspiring women join these groups more often than nonaspiring women? And how do the joining practices of aspiring and nonaspiring women stack up against the practices of seated men and women superintendents? Figure 4.9, "Membership in Professional Organizations," helps illustrate the answers to the questions posed.

Figure 4.9 uses data from the 2003 study (women assistant/associate/deputy superintendents or central office administrators and women superintendents), but for purposes of comparison and contrast, it includes data on men superintendents from the latest American Association of School Administrator's 10-year study of the American school superintendent (Glass, Björk, & Brunner, 2000). Several statements can be made. First, one association stands out as popular for all four groups—AASA or the American Association for School Administrators. This organization is the national association for superintendents. The membership of AASA includes a large number of central office administrators as well. One might assume that if anyone was interested in the superintendency, she or he would belong to this organization. The data support this assumption. The data reflect that, in terms of membership, women superintendents (78.6%) are at the top, followed closely by men superintendents (75.9%). In third place fall the aspiring

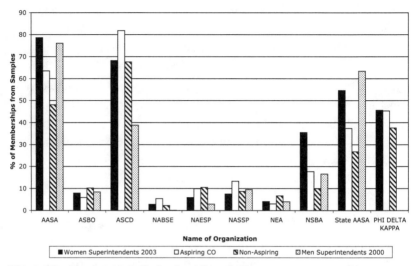

Figure 4.9. *Membership in Professional Organizations*

women (63.5%), and finally, at the low end are the nonaspiring women (48.1%).

Second, another popular association for the all women in the 2003 study is ASCD or the Association for Supervision and Curriculum Development. This fact is not surprising given that around half of the aggregate sample is made up of either current assistant/associate/deputy/directors of curriculum and instruction and/or women who have a background in elementary education. In the case of ASCD, 81.8% of aspiring women, 68.2% of seated women superintendents, and 67.6% of nonaspiring women are members. Interestingly, aspiring women top the list in terms of membership, even over women superintendents. This is not surprising, however, since half of all the assistant/associate/deputy superintendents are in charge of curriculum and instruction. Some women superintendents may drop this membership once in their positions due to time constraints. Perhaps most noteworthy is the stark contrast between the women and the men. Clearly, women overall are much more likely to join ASCD. In an age when academic achievement is at the top of every educators' agenda, these data may be another indication that women are more interested in curriculum and instruction and perhaps better prepared to lead our nation's schools.

Third, one organization stands out as the one that more men than women choose to belong—state-level AASA. These state-level associations are affiliates of the national level of AASA. Women superintendents belong to this organization at a much higher rate than do either aspiring or nonaspiring assistant/associate/deputy superintendents, with aspiring outnumbering nonaspiring again. This data is important for women who aspire. To be sure, whether male or female, seated superintendents find value in belonging to this organization. Aspiring women may want to heed this fact. Certainly, the state network is vital to any career move, and state-level organizations may make the difference between success or lack of success during a job search.

Fourth, one overall message is strong: Women who aspire to the superintendency join associations and organizations more often than do nonaspirants. Interestingly, however, 44.3% of nonaspirants evaluate nonuniversity-based professional development/training as "Very Useful" while only 36.3% of aspiring women find it "Very Useful." Clearly, the view that nonaspiring women hold of the development/ training offered through professional organizations and associations does not correspond as well as one would expect when considering their membership in the same organizations. Just the opposite is true for aspiring women; in contrast to nonaspiring women, a lower percentage of aspiring women believe that the development/training and perhaps networking opportunities offered through professional organizations is "Very Useful" and yet, a higher percentage of them, contrasted with nonaspiring, belong to these organizations and associations.

In fact, aspirants' membership practices more closely echo the membership practices of seated superintendents than do the practices of nonaspirants. In other words, there is evidence that women who aspire are willing to invest the time and energy to *belong to and spend time with* groups of people who hold positions to which the aspirants aspire. In fact, that may be the primary reason that aspirants join professional organizations. Aspirants step up to their next positions by networking and connecting with people who have already succeeded in this final career move. To continue the emphasis on their importance, the next subsection focuses on connections of a particular type, mentoring and role modeling.

Mentors and Role Models

Another form of professional education comes from mentoring or role models. Some of the questions in the 2003 survey asked about these forms of education. To illustrate the findings from these questions, we disaggregated the data by district size in order to determine if the size of the district limited or enhanced the availability of mentors and/or role models. In this case, we are also interested in whether women have same-sex mentors and/or role models.

Table 4.3 shows that the assistant/associate/deputy superintendents who are working in large districts have more experience working in districts headed by women superintendents than those working in small districts. The basic understanding for this question is that same-sex mentors and role models are important for anyone who aspires to climb the career ladder. Among all responses, the number who responded "Yes," meaning they have had experience working in districts headed by a woman superintendent, is roughly 30%. When we look across district size, however, the responses are more telling. While 41% of assistant/associate/deputy superintendents in large districts (more than 10,000 students) have worked in districts headed by women superintendents, as many as 79.5% of administrators from small districts have had *no* experience working in districts with women superintendents. It is safe to say that the chances are low that women in small districts will experience either same-sex role models and/or mentors within their own districts.

An additional question (Q039) asked the participants (of those who

Table 4.3.   Have You Ever Worked in a School District Headed by Female Superintendent?

District headed by female?	District Size				
	Less than 1,000	1,000–3,000	3,000–10,000	More than 10,000	Total
Yes	54(20.5)	90(27.9)	119(29.6)	123(40.9)	386(29.9)
No	209(79.5)	233(72.1)	283(70.4)	178(59.1)	903(70.1)
Total	263(100)	323(100)	402(100)	301(100)	1,289(100)

Note: x^2: 28.903 ****, df: 3. The value of x^2 is obtained from Pearson Chi-Square statistic.
*** $p<.001$. The figures in parenthesis indicate the percentage of that cell number.

had a mentor) whether their mentor was a practicing or retired superintendent who helped them get their jobs as assistant/associate/deputy superintendents. Around 60% of both aspiring and nonaspiring women responded to the question with "Yes, a practicing or retired superintendent helped me get my job."

Question 040, which followed the question above, asked, "Was the superintendent who helped you get a job and served as your mentor a male or female?" The responses for aspiring (Yes) and nonaspiring (No) were again disaggregated by district size. When comparing the aspiring and nonaspiring, we see that quite naturally both groups have a larger percentage of men mentors (61 to 67%) than women mentors. Further analysis reveals that those who aspire had a much greater percentage (24%) of *both* men and women mentors contrasted with the nonaspiring (12.4%). Perhaps the perspectives of both women and men mentors are important if women are to feel confident enough to aspire to the masculinized role of the superintendency. Clearly, a variety of mentoring plays an important part in career advancement.

Table 4.4. (Q040) Was the Superintendent Who Served as Your Mentor a Male or Female? With District Size. (Q105) Do You Aspire to the Superintendency?

Q105		District Size				
		Less than 1,000	1,000– 3,000	3,000– 10,000	More than 10,000	
YES	Q040 Male mentor?	1	17	35	31	84
		25.0%	68.0%	70.0%	67.4%	67.2%
	Female?	2	1	5	2	10
		50.0%	4.0%	10.0%	4.3%	8.0%
	BOTH	1	7	10	13	31
		25.0%	28.0%	20.0%	28.3%	24.8%
	Total	4	25	50	46	125
		100.0%	100.0%	100.0%	100.0%	100.%
NO	Q040 Male mentor?	9	32	68	42	151
		69.2%	80.0%	76.4%	61.8%	71.9%
	Female?	4	3	12	14	33
		30.8%	7.5%	13.5%	20.6%	15.7%
	BOTH	0	5	9	12	26
		.0%	12.5%	10.1%	17.6%	12.4%
	Total	13	40	89	68	210
		100.0%	100.0%	100.0%	100.0%	100.0%

MISCELLANEOUS DIFFERENCES

There are a few less interesting differences between the aspiring and nonaspiring women assistant/associate/deputy superintendents. This section will briefly highlight these contrasts.

First, when asked where they see themselves in 5 years, 71.9% of aspiring women answered that they would be "In a superintendency for the first time" (Q098, 2003 AASA survey). To the same question, obviously almost none (1.8%) of the nonaspiring women used this answer. Along the same line, 28.5% of aspiring women indicated that they were actively applying for a superintendency at the time of the survey, while only 0.3% of nonaspiring women had submitted applications. Evidently, a small number of the nonaspiring women were ambivalent about their aspirations. Finally, when asked "How many offers of a superintendency have you received?" 77.3% of aspiring women had zero offers. This difference could be related to the age differences between the two groups. The younger women (aspiring) would not have had enough time in their central office jobs to have the larger number of offers.

Second, the opinions of aspiring women about the status/prestige of the position of superintendent as educational/community leader are somewhat stronger than those of nonaspiring women. Of the aspiring women, 40.3% believe that the superintendency is increasing in importance and influence, while only 31.8% of nonaspiring women hold the same beliefs. This difference might indicate that achievement theory (McClelland, 1971), which advanced that individuals tend to hold three culturally based needs that determine future behavior—the need for achievement, power, and/or affiliation (Cavalier, 2000)—may help explain why women aspire to the superintendency. Clearly, if over 40% of women aspirants believe that the superintendency is increasing in importance and influence, they may be motivated by achievement, power, and affiliation.

Finally, it is important to note the primary reasons that nonaspiring women give for *not* aspiring to the superintendency. The top four reasons and the percentage of nonaspiring women who indicated them are as follows: (1) "I'm happy with my current position and have no interest in changing jobs" (58%); (2) "Politics of the job don't appeal to me" (43.7%); (3) "Too much stress" (32.4%); and much further behind (4) "Superintendent's salary is not high enough for the weight of the job" (21%). Interestingly, none of these reasons are related to childrearing or family responsibilities. Instead, these reasons are career focused—either in terms of work conditions and benefits or personal satisfaction with their current circumstances.

Thus, while nonaspiring and aspiring assistant/associate/deputy superintendents have much in common, they also differ in substantive ways. To be sure, given the limitations of these data, we cannot take into account whether sexism is a piece of why 60% of the women in our sample did not aspire beyond their top central office positions. Certainly, it is difficult to believe that this group of top women administrators lacks the motivation necessary to move into the superintendency. Therefore, we conclude that the differences identified in this chapter may be the primary reasons that 40% of our sample planned to take the road less traveled. The next section of the book describes the women who planned to and succeeded in gaining access to the less trodden path and were superintendents at the time they were surveyed.

POISED ON TOP

CHAPTER 5

Profile of Women Superintendents

Then took the other, as just as fair,
And having perhaps the better claim,
Because it was grassy and wanted wear;

—Robert Frost (1916, p. 9)

This chapter reports the data on women in the superintendency in general. All the data are from the 2003 AASA National Survey of U.S. Women Superintendents and Central Office Administrators. The latter have been dealt with in chapters 3 and 4. The data in this chapter are not disaggregated according to race or ethnicity. Chapter 6 provides a full picture of women of color in the superintendency.

This chapter generalizes women in the superintendency. We report these data in depth so that women superintendents can see whether they fit the current norms or whether, for one reason or another, their experiences make them anomalies. Women who may be considering the superintendency as a career goal will also be interested in this profile to see where they are in relation to the typical woman superintendent. Since this is the largest study of its kind in the history of women in the superintendency in the United States, these data give us the confidence to say that we now know who our women superintendents are, what their career paths were, what some of their strengths are, and what many of their concerns and challenges are. That said, understanding what makes a typical superintendent does not preclude any woman from doing it differently and being different. Perhaps knowing that one is outside the norm is also an incentive to reach the highest position in educational leadership. After all, leaders generally break the mold!

The profile is developed using the following survey categories: Personal and District Demographics; Career Path and Professional Development; The Search, Contracts, and Evaluation; Board Demographics, Dynamics, and Decision Making; Stress, Fulfillment, Prestige, and Challenges; and Open-Ended Questions.

PERSONAL AND DISTRICT DEMOGRAPHICS

Ninety-three percent of the respondents identified themselves as white, 4.4% black, 1.0% Hispanic, 1.2% Native American, 0.1% Pacific Islander, and 0.1% other. Seventy-six percent of the superintendents were married, 8% single, 13% divorced, 0.1% separated, and 2% widowed.

The state with the largest number of women in our sample was New York with just over 11% of the sample residing there. Another 8% of the sample lived in California. The rest of the population was spread across most other states.

Seventy percent of the women were 55 years old or under, with nearly 30% under 50. This suggests that women are gaining the superintendency earlier than believed. Most of the superintendents were employed in full-time administrative positions by the time they were 40, and more than a third of them were appointed to the superintendency by the time they were 45. However, another 30% became superintendents between the ages of 51 and 65. These facts illustrate that there is not a particular age by which women *should* have reached the position. The wide range in the ages at which women take their first superintendency speaks to the variety of experiences women bring to the position. Most women superintendents have served in at least four different positions before becoming superintendent, and over 90% of the women have served in more than one school district.

Seventy-seven percent of the superintendents had raised children at some point in their career or were raising children at the time of the survey. About 35% of these were raising children aged 20 or under when they first became superintendents. Although not all superintendencies are the same, the additional responsibilities associated with child rearing do complicate the position for a superintendent— especially for a woman superintendent, as the literature attests (see among others, Brunner, 2000; Chase, 1995; Grogan, 1996). The size, location, and political climate of the district influence the amount of time a superintendent must spend immersed in the daily routine, but for all superintendents, personal time is important to help keep a balanced perspective. Thus, it is important to know that there are a significant number of women superintendents who are managing family responsibilities as well as the demands of the position. To know that women superintendents can and do raise children while serving in the role makes the position more attractive to those who do not want to delay seeking a superintendency until their children are older, as 30% of the respondents reported doing.

Most superintendents served in rural or small-town districts, with 60% of the women serving in districts that were under 3,000 students. However, compared to the male sample[1] reported in the Glass, Björk, and Brunner (2000) national study, there were fewer women in small districts. Seventy-two percent of male superintendents served in districts with fewer than 3,000 students. And more than a quarter of the women respondents in 2003 (26%) served in districts of 5,000 or more students, compared to only 16% of male superintendents. These figures certainly call into question the long-standing belief that women serve primarily in small districts. Districts were spread across all regions of the United States. The largest numbers of women were in the Mid-East states and the Great Lakes.

Women reported making personal and family changes in their lives to accommodate the demands of the superintendency. The largest number, 30%, delayed seeking the position until their children were older. Nineteen percent stated that their spouse took a less demanding position or a job with greater flexibility, and 20% of women superintendents and their spouses were in a commuter marriage. Another 20% reported a variety of accommodations—the most common of which was divorce. Thirteen percent of women superintendents were divorced. There are no comparative numbers on divorce for men or for the general population of superintendents. Ninety-five percent of men are married compared to 76% of women, and 8% of women are single compared to 5% of men.

CAREER PATH AND PROFESSIONAL DEVELOPMENT

Prior to becoming a superintendent, over half (58%) of the respondents had been elementary teachers, and 48% had been elementary principals. Twenty-one percent had been middle/junior high school princi-pals, and the same number had been high school principals. Fifty-seven percent had been directors/coordinators and 56% associate/assistant superintendents. The most common career path to the superintendency was teacher/principal/central office administrator. However, 49% of the respondents did *not* follow that path. Seventeen percent were teacher, central office administrators, then superintendent, and 16% were teacher, principal, then superintendent. These figures again reinforce the notion that women do not have to follow norms established by their male counterparts in order to become superintendents.

As has been reported before, women superintendents spend longer in the classroom on average before becoming an administrator than men (Shakeshaft, 1999). Forty percent of male superintendents report 5 or fewer years in the classroom (Glass, Björk, & Brunner, 2000), whereas 41% of the women in this study spent at least 11 years in the classroom. An interesting comment from the open-ended section adds perspective to this point: "Women have greater patience and nurturing when deal-ing with students, parents, and school employees. A woman takes care of a classroom, a school, and a district as she would take care of her family" (1225).[2]

Women superintendents reported a wide range of teaching experi-ences, but more of them have taught at the elementary level than men (38% compared to 17%). Unlike their male counterparts, 66% of whom served as coaches, women superintendents report a wide variety of extracurricular activities. Women served as club advisors, class advi-sors, or newspaper/annual yearbook sponsors much more often than men did.

Women superintendents spent time as assistant principals at all levels and as principals at all levels. Thirty percent of the population reported that they started their administrative careers as assistant principals, but 27% actually started out as principals. Another 29% report that their first administrative position was as a director or coordinator. Thirty-five percent of these first-time administrative positions were in the ele-mentary setting, 19% in the high school, and 21% at central office. What these figures tell us is that women learn how to become leaders through many different roles. There is no one "right" way to do it. As

Grogan (1996) found previously, demonstration of leadership ability is possible in both supervisory and nonsupervisory positions.

Women who become certified and seek the superintendency gain their first position very swiftly (see Table 5.1). Fifty-seven percent were successful in *less than* a year of entering the pool, and another 16% took a year to secure their first superintendency. The average rate of securing a first superintendency was 2 years. Anecdotal evidence in the past has suggested that it takes women longer to reach the superintendency than men. These figures do not support this belief, although there are still many women who must persevere beyond the first year or two of actively seeking a position. Thirteen percent of the population took 4 or more years to get the job. And women of color take longer than white women to gain their first superintendency. Women of color are twice as likely as white women to have to wait 4 or more years. One reason some women do not move as fast as they might is expressed in this comment in the open-ended section of the survey: "Women wait too long before seeking the superintendency. They think one more year or another level will strengthen their goal" (473).

It is interesting to note the growing number of women who are serving in their second or third superintendencies. Twenty-four percent of the women in this study had served in more than one district as superintendent, and yet this number is much lower than that of the general population of superintendents, reported to be 44% by Glass, Björk, and Brunner (2000). However, only 10% of the general population of superintendents serve in more than one state, compared to 7% of the women. The profile of women superintendents is much closer to the norm in this respect. Serving in a different state can be very attractive,

Table 5.1. Length of Time Seeking Superintendency after Certification

Length of Time	Men—2000 %	Women—2003 %
Less than 1 year	56	57
1 year	16	16
2 years	12	10
3 years	5	4
4 years	3	4
5+ years	9	9

as respondents commented in the open-ended section of the survey, as long as there is portability of pension/retirement programs.

Related to the above is the fact that more men than women were appointed to the superintendency from outside the district—68% compared to 55%. Women were more likely than men to be appointed from the inside. Men also spent a longer time in the superintendency than women. Fifty-eight percent of male superintendents spent more than 7 years in the position compared to 31% of women in the 2003 study, a 6% increase over the number of women who had spent the same amount of time in the 2000 study. This fact leads us to believe that longevity in the superintendency increases as it becomes more "normal" for women to be viewed as superintendents. Only 13% of the nation's superintendents were women according to the Glass, Björk, and Brunner (2000) study, whereas the 2003 study has identified 18%. We can anticipate that as the numbers increase, the profile of men and women in the superintendency will become more alike in certain respects. Holding multiple superintendencies, remaining longer in the positions, venturing into more than one state to serve, and functioning as role models and mentors for aspiring superintendents are some of the ways women are likely to more closely resemble their male counterparts in the future. However, the findings from this survey lead us to believe that women bring very different strengths and priorities to the superintendency so that men's and women's profiles will never look exactly the same. As one superintendent commented in the open-ended section of the survey, "The increased focus on academics and accountability should make the job more attractive to more women who tend to have more focus on curriculum, teaching, and learning" (630).

As in previous studies, mentoring was identified in this study as especially important for women to reach the superintendency (see Gardiner, Enomoto, & Grogan, 2000). Seventy-two percent of women superintendents were mentored into the position of superintendent, compared to 60% who were mentored into the central office. These figures are encouraging, on the one hand. They attest to the fact that women are receiving mentoring from both men and women who have gone before. On the other hand, they illustrate how important it is to receive particular, targeted mentoring to reach the superintendency.

There were many comments about the need for mentoring on the open-ended section of the survey. As one woman put it, "We all need a stronger network, mentoring at all levels is extremely important" (939). To be mentored earlier in her career is certainly helpful for a woman but mentoring seems to be especially important for women to access the top position. Because of the dearth of women who have held the position, more women were mentored by men than by women (77% compared to 8%) with 14% reporting both male and female mentors.

Turning to degrees and professional development, of note is the fact that more women superintendents than men have doctorates (58% compared to 44%). This confirms a belief expressed in the open-ended comments: "It seems that women need a doctorate to compete effectively. I believe you will find (in CA) almost all female superintendents will have a doctorate, and more years of experience than men they competed against" (1199).

Women superintendents are also more up-to-date in their academic preparation than men. Almost half of the women (47%) received their highest degree within the past 10 years compared with 36% of the men. More than 40% of the men earned their highest degree 15 or more years ago. Perhaps because they are more recent graduates, more women than men believed that their graduate programs prepared them well for the superintendency (79% compared to 74%).

Women superintendents more often take advantage of professional development opportunities to stay abreast of current instructional developments in the field. Seventy-three percent of women superintendents participated in Association of Supervision and Curriculum Development–sponsored activities compared to only 38% of their male counterparts (see Table 5.2).

While it is not surprising that more women superintendents also have undergraduate degrees in education—58% compared to 24%—this fact is closely connected to the higher number of women who started out as elementary teachers. Indeed, 35% of women superintendents began their administrative careers in elementary schools compared to 24% of men, who generally began as assistant principals or principals in high schools (41% compared to 20%). Traditionally considered the best preparation for the superintendency, high school administrative experi-

Table 5.2. Professional Development Participation

Organization	General Population of Superintendents—2000 %	Women—2003 %
ASCD	38	73
AASA	62	73
State education agency	63	63
State AASA	61	48

ence and/or coaching at the high school level are encouraged. However, in this era of high-stakes testing and academic accountability, elementary experiences may provide a better grounding for a superintendent aspirant. Knowledge and understanding of how to build literacy and numeracy skills permeate the entire Pre-K–12 landscape. Moreover, elementary settings provide excellent opportunities for administrators to learn how to work with diverse parent and community groups who, at the time, are often much more involved in their children's education than they are later.

Women and men superintendents join similar professional organizations, but the numbers are different (see Table 5.3). The top four organizations preferred by men were, in order: American Association of School Administrators (AASA) (76%), state affiliate of the American Association of School Administrators (state AASA) (63%), Association of Supervision and Curriculum Development (ASCD) (39%), and

Table 5.3. Membership in Professional Organizations

Organization	Men—2000 %	Women—2003 %
AASA	76	76
AASA (state)	63	55
ASCD	39	68
NSBA	17	36
NASSP	10	8
ASBO	8	8
NEA	4	4
NAESP	3	6
NABSE	1	3
Other	17	46

National School Boards Association (NSBA) (17%). Interestingly, slightly more women join AASA (79%), and the second most popular organization for women was the ASCD (68%). Fewer women join their state AASA (55%) and twice as many women superintendents join NSBA (36%). Women of color's preferences are even more dissimilar. About the same number of women of color are members of AASA (80%), slightly fewer belong to ASCD (64%), significantly fewer belong to their state AASA (42%), and significantly more belong to NSBA (52%). Women of color also join the National Association of Black School Educators (40%). The most interesting differences are found between membership in the state AASA and in NSBA. These discrepancies seem to indicate that membership in the state AASA organization has less to offer women than it has to men and, vice versa, membership in NSBA has more to offer women than it has to men, and certainly more to offer women of color.

THE SEARCH, CONTRACTS, AND EVALUATION

Search firms play an important role in assisting or preventing women from gaining access to the superintendency (see Tallerico, 2000a & b). Search firms are gatekeepers that play a significant role in whether or not a woman even gets to be considered by a school board. Twenty-three percent of women superintendents were hired by districts that used professional search firms, compared to 17% of men. Male superintendents were more successful in districts where the search was managed locally (55% compared to 46%). State school board associations managed searches in which the same number of men as women superintendents were hired (19% and 20%, respectively). Professional search firms are more likely to represent women candidates well because they bring a national perspective to the search, and because they are more likely to be hired by wealthier districts where women's leadership is less of an anomaly in the community.

In a related question, respondents were asked whether there was an "old boy/girl network" in their state that helps individuals get superintendent positions. The way male and female superintendents answered this question provides a striking contrast. Forty-seven percent of the men answered yes, compared to 74% of the women. Women are likely to be much more sensitive to this question since they are relative newcomers to the superintendency and, unlike their male counterparts, women are more aware of the necessity of mentoring and sponsorship. Many women superintendents commented on the power of the old-boy networks in their responses in the open-ended section of the survey. A representative comment revealed that: "the good old boy network is alive and well and must be managed" (1332).

Two additional questions on the survey asked first about perceived barriers limiting women's career opportunities and then about factors perceived to advance women's careers. As might be expected, more women saw limitations than men did. According to women superintendents, the top five limitations were, in order, a lack of mobility of family members, school board members' perceptions that women are not good managers, school board members' perceptions that women are unqualified to handle budget and finances, school boards do not actively recruit women, and the lack of mentors and mentoring in school districts. Not having encountered such obstacles themselves, male superintendents were *not* in strong agreement on many of these limitations with the exception of lack of mobility of family members: 72% of men saw this as an important or somewhat important factor compared to 88% of women, and 60% of men thought that the perception that women will allow their emotions to influence administrative decision was an important or somewhat important limitation. Seventy-two percent of women thought the same, but it ranked sixth out of 12 possible factors. That such a large proportion of women superintendents—already successful in the position—were in strong agreement on these perceived limitations is curious. Is popular literature to blame? Are these pervasive myths? Do school board members regularly express such opinions? Do administrator preparation programs suggest these are true?

There was more agreement among male and female superintendents on what may help to advance women's careers in the superintendency. All six factors were considered by more than 80% of each population to be important or somewhat important factors. Ninety-seven percent of the women, on average, agreed on these strengths: interpersonal skills, responsiveness to parents and community groups, the ability to maintain organizational relationships, knowledge of the instructional process, knowledge of curriculum, and the emphasis on improving instruction, in that order. Moreover, 83% of the men, on average, concurred. Such consensus of opinion on matters specific to women in the superintendency is rare. We conclude that women superintendents have demonstrated such skills and knowledge, and that they have gained a positive reputation for doing so.

One further indicator of women's success in the position was the self-reported most recent evaluation rating received from their boards. Ninety percent of the women were rated excellent or good, just as 92% of the men were. In addition, 52% of women superintendents also regarded themselves as very successful in the position compared to only 43% of men. Men's views seemed to be more modest—providing an interesting contrast in gender stereotypical self-perception. Since more women than men believed themselves to be very successful, we conclude that they must have been able to deal more effectively with factors inhibiting their effectiveness. Their board ratings of excellent seem to confirm this. As one tongue-in-cheek comment from the open-ended section described it, "Despite the fact that we wear make-up, have our ears pierced, and don't play golf, we have the intelligence, judgment, and skills to be very effective superintendents" (1182).

Both men and women superintendents agreed, if relatively faintly, on the factors that most inhibited their effectiveness (see Table 5.4). They were asked to mark only the two most important. The top four, in order, were inadequate financing of schools, too many insignificant demands, state reform mandates, and board micromanagement. For women, the last two were tied in significance, but 6% more men thought state reform mandates were inhibiting. Only 21% of the women and 27% of the men marked this factor, leading us to believe that most superintendents feel they are dealing quite adequately with reform challenges. That fewer women marked it could be a result of women's knowledge and expertise in leading instructional reform. Thirty-five percent of women superintendents were hired as instructional leaders compared to 24% of men (see Table 5.5). In addition, 46% of women compared to 38% of men described their board's primary expectation of them to be educational leaders. This is in contrast

Table 5.4. Factors That May Inhibit Effectiveness

Factors	Men—2000 %	Women—2003 %
Inadequate financing of schools	45	43
Too many insignificant demands	38	37
State reform mandates	27	21
Board micromanagement	20	21
Too much added responsibility	14	13
Collective bargaining agreements	14	12
Board elections; changed expectations	9	9
Inexperienced, unqualified, or ill-prepared staff	9	10
Insufficient administrative staff	9	10
Difficult relations with board members	6	7
Other	4	4
District too small	4	4
Lack community support	3	2
Racial/ethnic problems	1	2

to 38% of men who were hired as managerial leaders compared to 24% of women. And 10% of women compared to only 3% of men are expected to lead reform (see Table 5.6). All these factors in the aggregate point to a considerable substantive difference in the profiles of men and women in the superintendency. Women are clearly carving out a niche as leaders of learning.

The length of job contract is more or less the same for women as it is for men, but women seem to do slightly better than the general population. Thirty percent of the general superintendent population receives a 1- or 2-year term compared to 24% of women. Thirty-one percent of women receive a 4- or more year contract compared to 26% of the general population. This suggests that women get good advice from their mentors about what length of time to negotiate. Unfortunately, the surveys do not go into all the possible kinds of negotiated contracts, and

Table 5.5. Primary Reason for Hire

Reason	Men—2000 %	Women—2003 %
Personal characteristics	42	32
Change agent	26	27
Instructional leader	24	35
Not sure	4	3
No particular important reason	3	3

Table 5.6.   Board's Primary Expectation of Superintendent

Expectation	Men—2000 %	Women—2003 %
Education leader	38	46
Manager leader	38	24
Political leader	13	11
Other	8	4
School reform leader	3	10
Community leader	*	4

*Data not collected in 2000.

the report of the 2000 survey does not give salary figures for the general population. The 2003 survey found that 34% of women were earning from $75,001 up to $100,000, and 27% were earning from $100,001 up to $125,000. However, a disturbing 15% of women were earning from $25,000 to $75,000. Since we have no national comparative figures for male superintendents, it is possible that men are earning similar salaries. If state figures are anything to go by, though, this seems unlikely (see Grogan & Brunner, 2005a). Also see below for respondents' comments from the open-ended section regarding pay inequities for women.

We are concerned that as women move into the superintendency on the strength of their deeper knowledge of the technical aspects of the job—delivery of curriculum, knowledge of teaching and learning, familiarity with children and families, and a persistence that is crucial for the success of reform movements, they will not be as well rewarded as the men who have gone before them. When skill and prowess in the superintendency were associated with back-room negotiations and political maneuverings, men were paid relatively well. Of even greater concern perhaps is that with the heightened public scrutiny and increased expectations of time on the job, no superintendent is compensated well by corporate standards.

BOARD DEMOGRAPHICS, DYNAMICS, AND DECISION MAKING

Women superintendents reported that they serve primarily under boards of five or seven individuals. Forty-seven percent of women superintendents had more than two women on their boards, compared to 36% of men. This helps to dispel some of the myths that women board members are not in favor of hiring women superintendents.

Only 65% of women superintendents had a high opinion of their board members, characterizing them as very well qualified or qualified to handle their duties. They were more critical of their board's capabilities than their male counterparts, more of whom (71%) characterized their board members as very well qualified or qualified to handle their duties. However, more women than men believed their boards to be active, aligned with community interests (71% compared to 66%), and only 7% of women saw their boards as not active, accepting of recommendations made by professional staff, compared to 13% of men. These differences might be traced back to the way superintendents work with their boards. Fifty percent of the general population of superintendents compared to 47% of women superintendents described themselves as initiating action to maintain district effectiveness, whereas 50% of women superintendents compared to 48% of the general population described themselves as serving as a professional advisor and presenting alternatives and consequences in an objective fashion. The more directive a superintendent is, the less likely he or she will notice the general abilities of the board members.

Male superintendents are also more likely to take sole responsibility for board member orientation (55% compared to 45%). This fact seems consistent with the more directive stance suggested above. Related to the notion of who develops policy and policy options in the district, nearly half of the male superintendents (44%) described themselves as developers of policy and policy options in the district compared to 35% of women superintendents. Almost equal percentages of men and women superintendents saw the task as a shared responsibility between board and superintendents (38% compared to 37%), whereas more women served under boards that were primarily responsible for the development of policy and policy options (12% compared to 7%).

An interesting contrast to the above beliefs is the difference in perception of male and female superintendents as to how often the board accepts their policy recommendations. Ninety-two percent of women superintendents believed their recommendations were accepted almost 100% of the time compared to 88% of the men. We speculate that since women are less often in the position of individually developing policy, their recommendations are more often accepted. What comes through in these multiple-choice questions regarding the way women super-intendents view the board is that they have some confidence in their ability to work with their boards. Interestingly, on the open-ended questions, a much more critical stance is taken, as is discussed below.

But board input into decision making is only one source of input, albeit an important one. Superintendents also seek citizen participation in district decision making, but women superintendents involve their communities more often than do men (73% compared to 68%). The majority of both men and women superintendents creates planning/advisory committees of citizens for the same issues in order of impor-tance: strategic planning, objectives and priorities for the school and district, fund-raising, school-based decision making, and program changes and new curricular programs being considered. The largest percentage point difference was noted in the category of program changes and new curricular programs. Fifty-one percent of women saw the importance of citizen input into this issue compared to 59% of the general population. A likely explanation for this is found in the greater expertise and knowledge of instructional matters women bring to the superintendency. Women superintendents are more likely to rely on committees of experts for advice and planning of new programs and curriculum than are men. A superintendent explained her strategy in the open-ended comments this way: "I take input from the group(s) who will be most affected by the decision and consult the experts . . . before deciding" (940).

One survey question focused on the emergence of special interest groups that pressure boards to make decisions favorable to their inter-ests. Responses to this question were similar among men and women superintendents. Nearly 60% of all superintendents reported that there has been an increase over the past 10 years. There are some differences in the type of interest group. More of the general population of superin-tendents experienced an increase in political community groups, in reli-gious groups, and in groups representing the private sector. Nearly a third of all superintendents reported an increase in community interest groups. Sixteen percent of the women superintendents checked the "other" category, indicating that the special interest groups in their communities had agendas different from those listed above. Those most frequently cited as other were athletics/sports-related groups.

When asked to identify the most difficult problem their board faced, more women superintendents than men saw their boards as under financial pressure (42% compared to 36%). More men saw their boards under community pressure (17% compared to 12%), and surprisingly few superintendents believed their boards' greatest difficulty was with internal board conflict (8% of women compared to 5% of men), although 17% of both populations ranked "understanding appropriate board role" as the biggest problem for the board. While the numbers are different, women have the same perspective about board difficulties as men overall. According to Glass, Björk, and Brunner (2000), the top three problems facing the board were financial pressure, community pressure, and understanding appropriate role, in that order. In the discussion on the open-ended questions, we report the respondents' general unhappiness with board roles and expectations.

Superintendents' perspectives on how much weight their board members give to information from particular groups were interesting. The general population thought that very great weight or considerable weight was given to the following top six groups, in order: district superintendent, principals, central office staff, parents, teachers, and the local power structure. Women superintendents also ranked those six groups as the most influential. There was more agreement among the women, however. For instance, 66% of women thought boards heard what parents had to say compared to 58% of the general population, 55% of women thought board members paid attention to teachers compared to 45% of the general population, and 31% of women thought students had considerable influence compared to 23% of the general population.

By taking into account to whom the superintendents paid attention, this difference in perception might be accounted for. Again, there was general agreement among superintendents as to the groups that wielded most influence with them (in order): principals, school board members, central office staff, fellow superintendents, and teachers. However, the perceptions differ markedly as to the value of input from the groups mentioned above. Considerably more women superintendents paid attention to teachers than the general population of superintendents

(83% compared to 72%), and to parents (69% compared to 59%), and to students (49% compared to 39%). These three groups (teachers, parents, and students) are evidently more important to women superintendents than they are to the general population. Likewise, women pay more attention to community groups. Forty-two percent of women superintendents give very great or considerable weight to information from community groups compared to 37% of the general population of superintendents.

STRESS, FULFILLMENT, PRESTIGE, AND CHALLENGES

The findings in this section are very interesting. Women superintendents experienced more stress than their male counterparts (68% say they are under very great or considerable stress, compared to 51% of men). Yet, 74% of women compared to only 56% of men reported feeling considerably self-fulfilled in the position. Moreover, 74% of women compared to 67% of men would choose a career as superintendent if they had to do it all over again. Finally, 64% of women compared to 60% of men see themselves continuing in a superintendency over the next 5 years.

Therefore, the experience of stress is not necessarily a deterrent. We discuss the concept of flow according to psychologist Mihaly Csikszentmihalyi (1990, 1997) in chapter 7. Women superintendents are obviously enjoying their work despite the stressful conditions under which they operate. Sometimes stress is associated with meeting challenges and bringing about meaningful change—creating a sense of purpose in the position. The findings here demonstrate clearly that the majority of women superintendents approached the position with energy and enthusiasm, ready to continue their efforts.

Like men, most women superintendents who moved to a second or third superintendency moved to a larger district (37% compared to 38%). Thirteen percent of women cited board elections as the main reason for leaving to take another superintendency compared to 9% of men. Interestingly, only 10% women compared to 15% men cited conflict with board members as the reason they moved on. We speculate that although women are critical of their board members' abilities as reported above, they are also more attentive to developing and maintaining organizational relationships, as noted earlier. Thus, women may be able to deal better with board conflict than are their male counterparts.

Men's and women's perceptions of the status/prestige of the position of superintendent as educational/community leader in their districts differed. Men were on the whole more pessimistic than women. Nineteen percent of men compared to 14% of women thought the position was decreasing in importance, 44% men compared to 40% women felt it had remained the same as 10 years ago, and 27% men compared to 34% women believed it was increasing in importance. There could be several sources of these attitudes. Forty-six percent of men had been superintendents for 10 or more years, compared to only 20% of women. These veteran superintendents served during a very different time in our history of U.S. education. Even 10 years ago, there was much less emphasis on accountability and standardized testing. Björk, Bell, and Gurley (2002) state that educational administrators have been promoted on their abilities to serve as managers and decision makers for most of the 20th century. Therefore, if the role is shifting to one that is more associated with student performance and instructional issues—as many of the findings in this study suggest—it is likely that the superintendents who have served the longest do not have the same prestige and influence they once had. According to this study, women superintendents are much more up-to-date in their academic preparation and more involved in professional development activities related to curriculum and instruction than their male counterparts. Thus, women superintendents may have more influence in their districts under current conditions than some male superintendents.

The final multiple-choice question on the survey asked respondents to rate 30 possible issues and challenges facing their district at the time. Answers to this question give us a clear picture of the kinds of districts women superintendents serve in. Women superintendents do not have a very different view than the general population of the major issues and challenges they face. The top ones for all superintendents are financing schools, assessing and testing for learner outcomes, accountability/credibility, and demands for new ways of teaching and operating programs. However, more women than the general population are concerned about all of these issues (see Table 5.4). This could certainly be a reflection of the intensifying of state and federal demands for accountability in the time span between 2000 and 2003. But it could also be that more women superintendents have firsthand knowledge of these challenges than men. Eighty-three percent of women superintendents compared to 86% of men believed that "changing priorities in the curriculum" was a challenge. It is likely that many women superintendents brought knowledge and expertise of curriculum issues to the superintendency, rendering this concern less pressing than others.

Beyond the top four, women are concerned with different issues than the general population. They are more concerned with recruiting teachers (84% compared to 80%), and less concerned with administrator/board relations (77% compared to 83%). They ranked programs for children at risk as a much higher concern than the general population did. Women seem to serve in districts where changes in societal values and behavioral norms were much less challenging than for districts in the general population (64% women compared to 77% general). At the same time, women were concerned about changing demographics and their effect on social-cultural issues such as race relations, integration, segregation, and immigration (56% women compared to 52% general). Women—and women of color, in particular—seem to be more sensitized to issues of race and ethnicity (see further discussion in chapter 6). Women also did not find parent apathy and irresponsibility about their children to be as challenging as the general population did (74% general compared to 61% women). Two further items show quite a discrepancy between the views of women and the general population. Women are not as concerned about board members—either the caliber of persons serving on the board or about the caliber of their responsibilities. (Sixty percent of women saw the former as a great or significant challenge compared to 65% of the general population, and 49% of women saw the latter as highly challenging, compared to 58% of the general population).

There are no comparative data in the report of the 2000 survey on the item of collaborating with parents on services provided to children. Women superintendents ranked this issue quite highly (63% saw it as of great significance or significant). The item was new on the 2003 survey.

Overall, women find plenty of challenges in the superintendency. However, on 16 of the 30 items, they were less concerned than the general population. This finding seems consistent with the finding above that the majority of women superintendents are highly fulfilled in the position. For them, challenges are to be met. Even very significant concerns can be dealt with if a superintendent has the energy and commitment to do so.

RESPONSES TO OPEN-ENDED QUESTIONS

There were eight open-ended questions on the 2003 survey. No previous AASA national survey of superintendents included these questions; thus, we have no comparative data. It is important to acknowledge that male superintendents could have responded in the same fashion to these questions. What follows, though, is the rounding out of the picture we have been building of women in the superintendency. These qualitative data help amplify some of the foregoing discussion and add some perspectives that were not gained through the multiple-choice questions. We designed the open-ended questions to provide superintendents an opportunity to express themselves more fully than they had been able to on the multiple-choice questions. We composed the questions based on our earlier studies and others' research on the superintendency and women in the superintendency. Two questions that add interesting dimensions to our knowledge of women superintendents were (1) What about the superintendency would you like to see change for it to be a more attractive position for you or others? and (2) What else do we need to know about women in the superintendency?

Answers to the first question range from the desire for a decrease in board micromanagement, more effective board training, and better governance models to salary increases, better benefits, and more financial incentives for being superintendent. Women also wanted increased funding for public education, a decrease in unfunded mandates, and more administrative support in the role. There were also wishes for fewer union/collective bargaining problems, but those comments were surprisingly few.

Board Issues

Twenty-five percent of women superintendents were critical of some aspect of the board of education. Several softened their comments with a reference to their own boards with whom they felt they had a good relationship. However, there was a general feeling of dissatisfaction with board training and the capacity and/or willingness of board members to understand their roles. For example: "[Need] for school board associations to clearly define the role of board members" (656), "Train board members so that they understand their roles and responsibilities" (1196), and "Clearer separation of [superintendent] role from that of school board—too many gray areas now" (28). Related to this is the strong desire for the elimination of board micromanagement. Comments ranged from "Less micromanagement from board members—this takes up an inordinate amount of time" (476), "Less micromanagement by BOE members, and more emphasis of same by the State Bd. Associations" (626), to "Stop micromanagement—keep board in the intended role" (735). In addition, there were many comments about the governance model itself. Concerns about the way board members are elected and on what platform surfaced. "[Need] professional school boards rather than elected positions" (936), "Not to be controlled by an uninformed board—needs to be criteria for board members" (979), and "Different governance. School boards are not efficient and are personal agenda driven" (1009). Superintendents also said, "Change governance" (1114), "Eliminate boards" (1069), and "The system of changing school boards and their role makes it difficult to sustain long-term initiatives" (1221).

Salary Increases, Including Better Benefits

Comments about salary or pay came from about 11% of the respondents. Superintendents said they would like to see "Reasonable expectations and increase in pay" (846), "Equity in salary and benefits for both genders" (1225), "Pay scale commensurate with CEOs" (1021), "More financial rewards" (1304), and "Either salary or tax credit or other monetary incentive" (955). Respondents pointed out that "The intense responsibility should mean higher salaries" (1323), and that

"Women's salaries need to be comparable to men's in the same position" (1084).

Funding for Public Education

Women superintendents (10%) expressed desires both for increased funding for public education and for a decrease in unfunded mandates. They also wanted more control over how funds are spent. Examples of their concerns include: "[Need] increased resources" (540), "I would like funding from the state to be stabilized and not become a political football every year" (60), "More resources to help with the overwhelming volume of work" (650), "Inadequate funding for rural schools is pervasive. We are invisible to the politicians" (689), "Less unfunded mandates and underfunded mandates for districts achieving well above the norm" (742), and "[Need] increase in funds that would provide quality staff & facilities so that superintendent can focus on teaching and learning—overall school improvement" (911).

Answers to the question of what else we need to know about women in the superintendency were varied. Some were directed specifically at gender issues and others provided more general advice for women in the role or contemplating the role. A few comments were directed to us as researchers—what we could investigate further or what AASA could do further.

Gender Issues

Thirty-seven percent of the respondents made comments about how women superintendents were different from men or about how the community/school board or other administrators and staff treated the women superintendent differently from the way they would treat a male superintendent.

A few women superintendents saw gender as a nonissue or a detractor. Such comments ranged from "All women superintendents are no more alike than all men superintendents are alike—the qualities I admire in my colleagues have little to do with gender" (28), "Females shouldn't concentrate on gender, but the qualifications that they have that make them a good leader. Focusing on gender can stifle effectiveness" (503), and "KNOW FINANCE! FORGET ABOUT GENDER BIAS" (uppercase on the original survey) (682).

However, many of the women who answered this question of what else we need to know about the superintendency within the context of gender remarked on the prevalence of bias or stereotyping. For example:

Every interaction as a leader with board members, fellow superintendents, contractors, sales personnel, etc. is all influenced by the fact that I am a female. My decisions seem to be more often questioned. I am rarely one to proclaim prejudice or bias, but I have found this to be true. (860)

We [women superintendents] continue to deal with gender bias issues internally & externally (with business, community, etc.). I have 12 members on the Superintendent's Cabinet (8 are women 4 are men) and even though more than 75% of our workforce of nearly 4,000 are women, the men are unhappy that there aren't more men at the senior management level. (1331)

The fact that you are a woman is the first thing others notice. The stereotypes are there, though people overcome them at varying rates. Unfortunately, some never overcome the stereotypes: not tough enough, emotional, not bright enough etc. (1355)

Some cautioned that sexism was alive and well.

We still encounter sexism; are viewed differently than male superintendents; work harder than male counterparts. (707)

Sexism still exists; it is more covert than when I occupied a "lesser position." I am still surprised at the number of men who call me "dear," "honey" and other diminutives. (875)

Regarding the good-old-boy system,

Many rural communities seem to resent women in these roles, especially if a good-old-boy network exists. Women usually are fair, do a good job and base decisions on children. (992)

It is hard for women to learn the superintendency without good mentors, the "boys' club" is hard to "crack." Good male mentors can be a great asset. (1029)

School Boards need to be open to leadership from women for the superintendency. As a woman administrator, I have always been a minority. This will not change unless the "good old boys" network is dissolved. Women are and can be effective leaders when provided the opportunities. (1176)

Many remarked on the fact that women must work harder than men do. Comments ranged from "We've come a long way but we still have to work harder and smarter than our male counterparts" (1141) to "Women in the superintendency must work harder than men to be considered proficient in the job" (1297) to "[Women superintendents] usually need to work harder and/or longer than their male counterparts, and accomplish more to be respected" (835).

In addition, there were many comments about the loneliness of the position, the attitude of other women, and the need for a support group or network of other women. Comments included: "It's lonely—other women are often jealous or resentful & undermine female superintendents' efforts" (1326), "It is very lonely & there is no one to discuss problems if you are in an isolated area. State meetings are helpful in having a chance to network" (1220), "It is lonely—You must be very careful with male colleagues for fear of misunderstanding of nature of relationship" (1272), and "Being a woman at this level can be lonely. The lack of other women to discuss issues with can often lead to isolation. Male superintendents are helpful, but are not always accepting of females" (1279).

Advice to Aspirants

The question of what else we need to know about the superintendency also prompted 11% of the superintendents to give advice to other women aspiring to the role. Many of these statements were unique, but the theme running through them was unmistakable. They were all designed to encourage others and to let them know they could be successful. For example,

The care of children and teachers are first. Organizational and business management is the form. Always—conservative knowledge presentation. No jeans! No dresses! Suits and systems! (1348)

To be in the superintendency, you must develop a "thick skin" and take criticism well. (1222)

Find ways to network other than on the golf course. (778)

[It's] important to be persistent and not become discouraged at rejection/failure. (1045)

Women must learn to be prepared to deal with nastiness. REAL nasty. (1115)

Women must know who they are—what they can do—when to be nurturers—when to be a hard-ass. Timing is important—be honest—be who you are—use the strengths you have—communicate—don't feel like you have to "boss" someone—work together—but make clear who will make the tough call in a pinch. (1146)

And finally, in line with the findings from the multiple-choice section, women remarked on how much they enjoyed this work. They encouraged others to "Go for it!" (1329), said that "It is hard work but oh so fulfilling" (846), "It's a great job for a woman—lots of opportunity to accomplish great things" (1008), "It is truly a labor of love" (1236), and "Best job in the universe! Love it!" (589).

ENDNOTE

1. All comparisons to male superintendents or to the general population of superintendents are from Glass, Björk, and Brunner's *Study of the American Superintendency* (2000). We have provided comparative data on men superintendents when the data were disaggregated by gender in the 2000 study. When disaggregated data were not reported, we provided comparative figures from the general population of superintendents in the 2000 study.

2. Numbers following direct quotations from the survey refer to the individual whose survey was coded with that number.

CHAPTER 6

Women of Color in the Superintendency and Assistant/Associate/Deputy Superintendency

Oh, I kept the first for another day!
Yet knowing how way leads on to way,
I doubted if I should ever come back.

—Robert Frost (1916, p. 6)

This book is devoted to creating a sharper, more vivid image of women in senior educational leadership positions in the United States today. To do justice to this intention, it is important to provide a focus on women of color in these positions. This chapter is centered on the experiences, thoughts, and beliefs of the women of color in comparison to their white counterparts. Much of the earlier research on women in educational leadership has reported white women's stories with some attention to the circumstances of women of color. Some recent national studies, such as Glass, Björk, and Brunner's (2000) *The Study of the American School Superintendency,* included chapters on superintendents of color. However, the samples have been very small and, in many cases, since people of color have been a small portion of the population to begin with, no attention has been paid to creating a profile of women of color.

For some time, scholars have bemoaned our serious lack of knowledge of the lives and behaviors of women of color educational leaders. Literature devoted solely to research and discussion of women of color in educational leadership is thin but growing (see Ah Nee-Benham & Cooper, 1998; Alston, 1999, 2000, 2005; Brunner & Peyton-Caire, 2000; Dillard, 1995, in press; Enomoto, Gardiner, & Grogan, 2000; Grogan, 2000; Henry, 2000; Jackson, 1999; Murtadha-Watts, 2000;

Mendez-Morse, 1999, 2000, 2003, 2004; Nozaki, 2000; Ortiz, 1999, 2000, 2001; Ortiz & Ortiz, 1995; Sanders-Lawson, Smith-Campbell, & Benham, 2006; Simms, 2000; Tallerico, 2000a & b).

Drawn from the data on the 2003 survey, this discussion will be organized around the multiple-choice categories of Personal and District Demographics; Career Paths and Professional Development; the Superintendent Search, Contracts, and Evaluation; Board Dynamics and Decision Making; the Challenges and Fulfillment of Upper-Level Administrative Leadership, Including the Superintendency; and Responses to the Open-Ended Questions on the survey.

PERSONAL AND DISTRICT DEMOGRAPHICS

The profile of women of color at the senior level of educational administration in the United States is different from the one of their white counterparts. A total of 102 members of nonmajority racial/cultural groups answered the 2003 survey. Seven women did not give their position; therefore, the data are based on the other 95 respondents. Fifty of these women were superintendents, and 45 were assistant, associate, or deputy superintendents. Of the 95, 65% identified themselves as black, 17% as Hispanic, 13% as Native American, 2% as Asian, and 1% as Pacific Islander. Almost half of the group (49%) was between 51 and 55 years old. The majority of this group (64%) was first employed in a full-time administrative position before the age of 35.

The women of color were younger than the white women. More than twice as many white superintendents were 56 or older (31% compared to 14%). In addition, three times as many white central office administrators were 56 or older (28% compared to 9%). However, it takes women of color longer to become superintendents than it does white women. Thirty-six percent of white women had become superintendent by age 45 compared to 28% of women of color.

Fewer women of color administrators were married than white, senior-level women administrators (65% compared to 76%). And 20% of senior-level, women administrators of color were divorced compared to 13% of senior-level, white women administrators. Interestingly, there was little difference among superintendents: 72% of women of color superintendents were married and 76% of white women superintendents were married. On a related issue, nearly a quarter of white women superintendents reported not raising and never having raised children, while only 12% of the women of color superintendents reported the same. Moreover, 32% of women of color superintendents were raising or had raised three children or more compared to 23% of white women superintendents.

While the women of color senior-level administrators, like their white counterparts, are found in all kinds of districts across the country, there were many more women of color superintendents in urban districts than white women—nearly four times as many (27% compared to 7%). Forty-eight percent of white women superintendents were in suburban or suburban rural districts compared to 37% of the women of color. Similarly, there were nearly four times as many women of color central office administrators in urban settings than white women (40% compared to 11%). And more women of color served in districts of 10,000 or more students than do white women (35% compared to 21%). Nearly half the women of color central office administrators were in districts of 10,000 or more students, compared to only a third of white women. One further point needs to be made about the kinds of districts in which women of color serve. Only one third of white women superintendents are in districts with declining enrollment compared to 42% of women of color superintendents.

Where are the greatest numbers of women of color to be found? The majority are in the Great Lakes, the South East, and the South West. White women superintendents are mainly in the Great Lakes, and Mid-East with representation in all other parts of the country, including Alaska. In the central office, women of color are also to be found mainly in the South East and South West.

CAREER PATHS AND PROFESSIONAL DEVELOPMENT

Looking at the career paths of the women of color superintendents compared to the white women superintendents, we find that twice as many women of color have held elementary assistant principalships as have white women superintendents (see Table 6.1). Also, more women of color superintendents have held junior high/middle school assistant principalships and more women of color superintendents have held elementary principalships than have white women superintendents (58% compared to 48%). About the same percentage of women of color as white women superintendents have held high school principalships (22% compared to 21%). When we add the figures of women of color central office administrators, it becomes clear that, in general, women of color serve more often in principalships than white women. Twice as many women of color central office administrators have held junior high/middle school assistant principalships and principalships, more have held elementary principalships (47% compared to 38%), more have held high school assistant principalships, and twice as many have held high school principalships (29% compared to 11%).

Women of color superintendents have also served more often as director/coordinator and assistant superintendent than have white women superintendents. In sum, there seem to be more hoops for women of color to jump through on their way up the administrative career ladder than for white women. On average, white women described having had experience in four different administrative areas, compared to five or six for women of color. Fifty-six percent of women of color superintendents compared to 50% of white women served as teachers, principals, and central office administrators before becoming superintendents. Sixty-four percent of women of color central office administrators were teachers and principals compared to only 47% of white women central office administrators. It is much easier for white women to be promoted

Table 6.1.   Career Path to the Superintendency

Career Path	% Women of Color Superintendents	% White Women Superintendents
Teacher/principal/central office	56	50
Teacher/central office	20	17
Other	10	11
Teacher/principal	8	17
Principal/central office	6	1
Teacher only	0	2
Central office only	0	1
Principal only	0	<1

into the central office from a teaching position than it is for women of color.

Interestingly, however, women of color were tapped for administration earlier than their white counterparts. About one third of the total population of women of color left classroom teaching for an administrative position after 5 years, compared to only 19% of the white population (see Table 6.2). Twenty-seven percent of women of color senior-level administrators taught for more than 10 years, compared to 43% of white women.

Women of color had a slightly better chance of being appointed to the superintendency from outside than white women (60% compared to 55%). Women of color central office administrators were also more prepared to enter the superintendency. Eighty-five percent of them already have or are working on their superintendency certificate, compared to 73% of white women. However, as mentioned above, it takes longer for women of color to get a superintendency than it does for white women. Forty-seven percent of women of color gained the position less than a year after they were certified and sought the position, compared to 58% of white women. And women of color are twice as likely as white women to wait 4 or more years for a superintendency.

It is interesting to note that more women of color senior-level administrators had worked in districts headed by women than had white women (38% compared to 28%). Moreover, 45% of women of color central office administrators had worked under a female superintendent, compared to 36% of white women. This suggests an interesting connection to the figures on aspiration. Fifty-nine percent of women of color assistant/associate/deputy superintendents aspired to the superin-

Table 6.2. Number of Years as a Classroom Teacher for Women Administrators

Years	% Women of Color	% White Women
0	2	4
1–5	33	19
6–10	38	34
11–15	21	27
16–20	3	12
21–25	3	3
26+	0	1

tendency, compared to 37% of white women in those positions. One plausible explanation for the difference is that women of color had had more opportunity to imagine themselves in the position because they had had female role models.

On a related note, though, only 52% of the women of color central office administrators had had mentors or mentoring, compared to 72% of the women of color superintendents. This suggests that it is very hard for women of color to make the leap into the superintendency. Mentoring was also an issue for white women. Sixty percent of white women in central office reported having been mentored, compared to 72% of white women superintendents. We can conclude that, while it is helpful for women to be mentored into central office, it is almost necessary to get mentoring to reach the top job. The difference in the rate of mentoring for women in central office compared to the rate of mentoring for women superintendents underscores the importance of mentoring for all women aspirants to reach the superintendency, as mentioned more fully elsewhere in this book.

In general, women of color were better educated than white women. Of the total population, 61% of women of color had doctorates compared to 52% of white women. And 54% of women of color received their highest degree in the past 10 years compared to 45% of white women. While there were not many women in senior-level administration working on an academic degree at the time of the survey, there were almost twice as many women of color working on one as white women (16% compared to 9%). These figures suggest that it is more important for women of color than for white women to have all the formal qualifications, such as degrees and certification, before they seek the superintendency.

There were some differences in the sources of professional development for women of color superintendents compared to white women superintendents. More women of color attend professional development training held by the National School Boards Association (NSBA) than white women superintendents (64% compared to 43%). By contrast, more white women superintendents attend state American Association of School Administrators (AASA) professional development (49% compared to 38%), and they attend training offered by state education agencies more often than women of color superintendents do

(64% compared to 48%). These preferences are linked to membership in the above organizations. Fifty-two percent of women of color superintendents, compared to 34% of white women superintendents, belonged to NSBA. Fifty-six percent of white women superintendents belonged to their state AASA organization, compared to 42% of women of color superintendents.

On the national scene, many more women of color superintendents have attended the annual AASA conference than white women superintendents (69% compared to 46%). And 45% of women of color central office administrators attended the same conference, compared to 34% of white women central office administrators. Similarly, 28% of women of color superintendents and 22% women of color central office administrators have attended the AASA Women's Conference, compared to 17% of white women superintendents and 12% of white women central office administrators. Clearly, these national conferences offer more support for women of color than state-level conferences where the numbers of women of color in educational administration are much fewer.

THE SUPERINTENDENT SEARCH, CONTRACTS, AND EVALUATION

Related to the above is the finding that fewer women of color superintendents were hired in districts that used the state school board association to manage their search (13% compared to 20% of white women superintendents). More women of color were hired by districts that used professional search firms (36% compared to 22%).

Given the general picture of women of color encountering more obstacles as they make their way into and through the yellow wood, it is not surprising that they saw more factors limiting opportunities for women superintendents or women aspiring to the superintendency. Eighty-six percent of women of color superintendents compared to 73% of white women superintendents felt that the tendency of school boards not to actively recruit women was an important or somewhat important factor (see Table 6.3a). More of them also believed that there is a midmanagement career "glass ceiling" (87% compared to 67%). Women of color central office administrators had a similar belief (91%

compared to 73%; see Table 6.3b). Seventy-seven percent of women of color superintendents compared to 62% of white women superintendents believed there is a lack of opportunities to gain key experiences prior to seeking the superintendency. Women of color central office administrators agreed (80% compared to 62% of white women in central office). Another area of concern was the lack of professional networks. Eighty-four percent of women of color superintendents and 91% of women of color central office administrators felt this was a barrier, compared to 69% of white women superintendents and 64% of white women central office administrators. These figures clearly indicate that the available professional networks are primarily helpful for white women educational administrators. Closely related was the belief that there is a general lack of mentors or mentoring for women of color (86% of the total women of color population compared to 69% of the total white population).

The difference in lived experiences obviously accounts for another major difference in the way women of color senior-level administrators view the yellow wood compared to the way white women do. Sixty-one percent of the women of color saw discriminatory hiring and promotional practices as a major problem limiting administrative career opportunities for individuals of color; only 20% of the white women saw it similarly.

Table 6.3a. Perceived Barriers Limiting Administrative Opportunities for Women Superintendents

Barriers	% Women of Color	% White Women
Lack of mentors/mentoring	90	71
Midmanagement career "glass ceiling"	87	67
School boards do not actively recruit women	86	73
Lack of professional networks	84	69
Board members' perception of women's ability to handle finance and budgets	83	77
Lack of mobility of family members	79	89
Lack of opportunities to gain key experiences	77	62
Board members' perception of women as managers	76	79
Perception that women will allow emotions to influence decisions	76	71
Nature of work makes it an unattractive career	69	70
Perception that women are not politically astute	67	58
Perception that instructional emphasis limits administrative skills	64	57

Table 6.3b. Perceived Barriers Limiting Administrative Opportunities for Women Central Office Administrators

Barriers	% Women of Color	% White Women
Board members' perception of women as managers	96	82
Midmanagement career "glass ceiling"	91	73
Lack of professional networks	91	64
Lack of mobility of family members	89	78
Board members' perception of women's ability to handle finance and budgets	89	74
Perception that women are not politically astute	87	60
Perception that women will allow emotions to influence decisions	84	73
Lack of mentors/mentoring	82	65
Lack of opportunities to gain key experiences	80	62
Perception that instructional emphasis limits administrative skills	78	62
School boards do not actively recruit women	71	74
Nature of work makes it an unattractive career	66	60

There is a clear connection between the presence of individuals of color on a board and the likelihood of women of color being hired. Sixty-nine percent of women of color were hired by boards with at least one person of color on the board compared to 24% of white women. Thirty-one percent of women of color were hired by boards with four or more board members of color compared to only 2% of the white superintendents. More than twice as many white women superintendents as women of color superintendents served under all white boards.

When asked what was the most important reason the board selected them, significantly more women of color superintendents believed they were hired to be change agents (41% compared to 25% of white women superintendents). And 25% of the women of color superintendents compared to only 9% of white women superintendents were primarily expected to lead reform in their districts. Board micromanagement was perceived as an inhibitor to the superintendent's success by twice as many women of color superintendents (40% compared to 19%). On a related note, only 57% of women of color superintendents were rated "excellent" compared to 71% of their white counterparts. And more than three times as many women of color superintendents as white women superintendents have not been evaluated. This lack of feedback in general, and of positive feedback in particular, surely serves to frustrate women of color superintendents.

However, women of color appear to be getting paid well for their hardships. Nearly twice as many women of color superintendents as white women superintendents were earning between $125,000 and $150,000 (24% and 13% respectively). And 38% of women of color superintendents were earning $125,000 or more, compared to 23% of white women superintendents. The very best salaries, though, are reserved for white women superintendents. One percent of the white population was earning $200,000 or more compared to none of the women of color superintendents.

BOARD DYNAMICS AND DECISION MAKING

Considering the above, it is not surprising that white women superintendents had a higher opinion of board members than women of color superintendents did. Sixty-six percent of the former compared to 49% of the latter believed that board members are very well qualified or qualified to handle their duties. This could be a result of the way women of color superintendents characterized their board members. Nearly twice as many of them described their board members as representing distinct factions in the community and voting accordingly (32% compared to 19%). Many more white women superintendents saw their board members as active, aligned with community interests, but not rigid (72% compared to 55%). Related to board issues is the development of district policy and policy options. More white women superintendents reported that the superintendent develops policy and policy options than women of color superintendents (36% compared to 25%). Over a third of both groups believed that developing policy is a shared responsibility between boards and superintendent.

The respondents were sharply divided over perceptions of the emergence of interest groups in districts over the past 10 years. Seventy-one percent of the women of color superintendents reported that there were interest groups in their districts pressuring the board to make decisions favorable to their group. Only 58% of the white women superintendents reported the same. An even greater difference was noted among women central office administrators: 89% of women of color reported the presence of interest groups compared to 70% of the white women.

The interest groups were identified as one of the following: political, religious, or community. All the respondents agreed that the majority of the interest groups were community interest groups, suggesting interest issues around race, ethnicity, and/or language. The difference in the women of color's perceptions compared to white women's perceptions of the presence of interest groups could be accounted for by the differences in the kinds of districts in which the respondents served.

On a related question, respondents were asked what they considered the most difficult problem their board members faced as board members. The majority of answers were spread across three areas: financial, community pressure, and understanding the role of a board member. Nearly half the white women superintendents chose financial. About a quarter of the women of color checked financial, a quarter checked understanding the role, and another quarter checked community pressure. In fact, twice as many women of color checked community pressure as white women did (24% compared to 12%). The fourth quarter of women of color was distributed across all other possible answers.

One reason for women of color superintendents' heightened sensitivity to community-based interest groups and community pressure on the board can be found in the extent to which superintendents reported involving parents and citizens in a planning/advisory capacity in their school districts. More women of color superintendents involved citizen groups in these activities than white women superintendents did. The exceptions were in the area of finance and budget where slightly more white women superintendents involved parents/citizens, and in the area of fund-raising where the numbers are the same (see Table 6.4).

One final indicator of women of color's experiences with special interest groups and board members was the response to a question asking the women to indicate how much weight they believe board members give to various individuals/groups. Little difference was found in the way the majority and minority superintendents responded except for the weight they gave to community groups and to the power structure in the community. Nearly half the women of color believed that board members give very great weight or considerable weight to the former compared to only 29% of white women superintendents, and slightly over half of the women of color believed board members give very great or considerable weight to the local power structure in the

Table 6.4. Areas in which Superintendents Involve Parents/Citizens in a Planning Advisory Capacity in Their School District (2003 Survey)

Areas of Involvement	% Women of Color Superintendents	% White Women Superintendents
Strategic planning	78	65
Objectives and priorities for school and district	71	65
Fund-raising	63	63
School-based decision making	61	52
Student behavior	57	42
Program changes and new curriculum	53	50
Student activities	51	43
Evaluation of programs	41	30
Finance and budget	35	38

community compared to 37% of white women superintendents. Women of color superintendents also reported that, as superintendents, they place more weight on information from community groups than their white counterparts (56% compared to 41%; see Table 6.5). They also listened more to parents (79% compared to 68%), students (63% compared to 48%), and the local power structure (45% compared to 33%).

Clearly, for whatever reason, women of color superintendents dealt more often with community groups that represent race, ethnicity, or linguistic concerns. A variety of questions on the survey contribute to

Table 6.5. Sources of Information for Superintendents

Sources	% Women of Color Superintendents	% White Women Superintendents
School board members	96	94
Principals	94	93
Central office staff	91	89
Teachers	87	83
Fellow superintendents	87	77
Parents	79	68
Students	63	48
State office staff	63	47
Community groups	56	41
Power structure in the community	45	33
Consultants	42	40
Professional organizations (e.g., AASA)	35	35

this overall picture. It is not clear whether women of color are more likely to be appointed in multiethnic districts or whether, once appointed, community groups form. Such groups might form either because they feel supported by a superintendent of color or because they feel threatened by a superintendent of color, and formation might depend on which ethnic group the superintendent of color represents. In any case, community groups interact much more often with women superintendents of color than with white women superintendents.

No doubt the tension and conflict resulting from dealing with this pressure takes a toll on women of color superintendents. Fewer of them saw themselves continuing as superintendent in the next 5 years (53% compared to 65% of the white women superintendents). While there were not many respondents who saw themselves taking early retirement, it is perhaps significant that twice as many women of color superintendents checked that box than white women superintendents (14% compared to 7%).

In contrast, 42% of women of color central office administrators saw themselves in a superintendency for the first time compared to 29% of white women. This confirms the differences in aspiration between the two groups. Fifty-nine percent of the women of color central office administrators indicated that they aspired to the superintendency, compared to 37% of the white women in that population. Moreover, 40% of the former group was actively seeking a superintendency at the time of the survey, compared to 28% of the latter. For whatever reason, women of color have more drive to reach the superintendency than white women do.

Respondents who did not aspire to the superintendency gave several reasons for why they did not aspire; however, no strong difference between the majority and nonmajority groups emerged. In fact, none of the reasons given, such as lack of mobility, lack of administrative experience or academic training, having to take a cut in salary, and so forth, garnered much response at all. Only two reasons seemed to strike a chord with the respondents. One was the unappealing politics of the job, and the other was satisfaction with a current position. Twenty-two percent of women of color compared to 28% of white women checked the former, and 24% of women of color compared to 37% of white women checked the latter. In the first instance, because fewer women of color than white women were deterred by this factor, we speculate that women of color may be already socialized into the kind of politics with which they will have to deal. As already noted, more of the senior central office administrators of color had been principals or assistant principals than the white women senior central office administrators.

THE CHALLENGES AND FULFILLMENT OF UPPER-LEVEL ADMINISTRATIVE LEADERSHIP, INCLUDING THE SUPERINTENDENCY

Not surprisingly, fewer women of color reported being satisfied with their current jobs as a reason not to aspire to the superintendency. Women of color in senior central office positions, like women of color superintendents, reported having to deal with community pressure groups more than white women did. They described more challenges in general than white women did. Thus, being satisfied with their current position was not likely to be a reason for them to reject the superintendency. Women of color central office administrators may have been satisfied with their positions or they may not have been. Their jobs were already steeped in considerable conflict so it is possible that the desire to have the power of a superintendent to deal with the issues would motivate them to aspire to the superintendency.

Consistent with this idea was the higher confidence in the status of the superintendent reported by the women of color superintendents. Forty-five percent of women of color superintendents compared to 33% of white women believed that the status/prestige of the superintendent as educational/community leader in the district was increasing in importance and influence compared to 10 years ago. This confidence no doubt encouraged more women of color to aspire to the position than white women.

The final multiple-choice question on the survey revealed differences similar to those already discussed between the kinds of districts women of color superintendents served in compared to those of white women. Asked to rate the importance of 30 issues and challenges they were facing as superintendent, respondents thought alike on two thirds of the issues. They differed to the extent of more than 10 percentage points on the following nine challenges: the significance of changing demographics and their effect on sociocultural issues such as race relations, segregation, and immigration; changing priorities in the curriculum; caliber of persons assigned to or removed from local boards of education; affirmative action programs/Title IX; student discipline and gangs; strategic planning and mission statements; developing and funding institutional programs for children at risk; parent apathy and irresponsibility about their own children—including child abuse; and school-based decision making (see Table 6.6).

Worthy of note is that more superintendents of color believed these challenges to be of great significance or significant, with the exception of changing priorities in the curriculum. However, what is most striking is the clear difference of opinion on these nine issues. These differences in opinion confirm the fact that superintendents of color serve in quite different kinds of districts than do white women and that they are more sensitive to certain challenges than are white women. Changing demographics, affirmative action programs, student discipline problems, and the need to develop and fund programs for children at risk are more likely to be of greater concern in districts with distinct ethnic communities with a range of socioeconomic levels where women of color are more likely to serve, than in more homogenous, wealthier districts where white women are more likely to serve. Moreover, the lived experiences of women of color make it much more likely that they will pay attention to these challenges.

Table 6.6. Issues and Challenges Facing the Superintendency Today in Their School District (2003 Survey)

Challenges Faced	% Women of Color Superintendents	% White Women Superintendents
Strategic planning and mission statements	83	68
Developing and funding programs for children at risk	81	70
Caliber of persons assigned to/removed from local boards	74	59
Parent apathy and irresponsibility	72	61
Changing priorities in the curriculum	71	84
Changing demographics	71	54
School-based decision making	63	39
Student discipline, gangs	53	32
Affirmative action programs/Title IX	47	18

Similarly, we can couple issues of decision making, quality of board members, strategic planning, and parent apathy as indicative of the challenges identified earlier by women of color superintendents. These superintendents appear to deal more often with contentious community issues and do not always have confidence in the board's ability to behave in a nonpartisan manner.

OPEN-ENDED QUESTIONS

At the end of the survey were a number of questions aimed at understanding a little more about what it is like to be a senior-level educational administrator. Most relevant to this chapter was the question: If you are a woman of color, how do you feel your experience as a woman of color in a leadership position has differed from others' experiences? Exactly what makes it different and how have you dealt with it?

Superintendents' Comments

The responses from the superintendents were a little different from the central office administrators' responses. Superintendents wrote about (a) overcoming perceptions, (b) overcoming institutionalized racism and sexism, and (c) community relationships.

Overcoming Perceptions

The superintendents discussed what they had to overcome to reach the position and what they still encounter. There was a strong sense of having to prove oneself. Two comments below are typical of this kind of remark.

It took two years of success to be included unconditionally. (1348)

As a woman of color, I feel the need to excel and prove to others that I can be more successful than others. The ability of a white male is not automatically questioned. (838)

Related to these comments were those that mentioned higher expectations and heightened accountability.

The expectations are higher and the tools are not as available as for white counterparts. (1240)

May be an expectation that I work harder and perform twice as well. (1248)

Some comments drew attention to how it feels to be either the object of a lot of critical attention or to be overlooked—the sensation of being in a fishbowl or being invisible in a majority white community.

Leaders of color are scrutinized and second-guessed more. (1342)

A woman of color always has to do a better job; there is little room for error; her actions are watched and evaluated more closely. (1203)

Many times you are overlooked in the white community, particularly with white males. You are treated as invisible. I focus on the work and I also hired a deputy to interface with that segment of the community. (846)

The third comment suggests the need for political strategizing to deal with this sensation. Many white superintendents have done the same—hired members of diverse communities to be the liaison with that community. However, unlike the white superintendent who is often seen as sensitive to the particular community, the superintendent of color runs the risk of making herself irrelevant to the white community who will go around her to deal with the white deputy.

As another superintendent put it, "When you look at me what do you see? A mother, a laborer, or a professional. I believe that women of color do not fit the white balding male standard [administrator]" (1005).

Overcoming Institutionalized Racism and Sexism

Women of color superintendents felt that they were operating on an unequal playing field with white men and women. They commented on both racism and sexism and the tensions created by the intersection of both. The following examples reflect the harder road to the superintendency that was clear in the multiple-choice responses.

Advancement slower, more risk taking and leading complex projects. (1248)

Really I think the issue is gender more than race. (772)

As a Spanish person I felt the pressure of the "glass ceiling" when I reached for the Assistant Superintendency—I received "1" ratings but not the job—it was a hard search—I'm glad I did not give up. The super-intendency was easier—I received two offers on my first search. (1266)

This last comment is instructive. While there was no question on the survey that pinpointed the difficulty of securing an assistant/associate/ deputy superintendency, there are many anecdotes and some research to indicate that those positions can function as gatekeepers, particularly for individuals from outside the district.

Community Relationships

Consistent with the findings from the multiple-choice questions, women of color superintendents commented on the difficulties associ-ated with being seen as "different" in the wider community. Just as they are seen to be an anomaly within the district organization, they are objects of curiosity and skepticism in the suburbs or cities where they work. Sometimes the issue is gender more than race, as this comment below illustrates.

As the first Native American women superintendent of a public school on my Indian Nation, the challenges are greater than the principalship. The differences range from being articulate in two languages while working with two cultures, to cultural male beliefs of women in a leader-ship role (Indian women should stay home and raise children). (1225)

Sometimes race or ethnicity is the issue: "Being a superintendent in the community in which I live makes it very difficult for community persons to give respect for the person in the position" (1083).

Two comments indicate that turning it into the "other's" problem is an effective way of dealing with it.

It's no different than being the "only one" of color in other settings— theater, restaurant, college classroom etc. It's who you are with pride and it's the other person's adjustment. (673)

Communities and the Board of Education are not comfortable with females of color in leadership positions. I deal with it by leaving the issue with them and not taking it as my own. (549)

Central Office Administrators' Comments

The assistant/associate/deputy superintendents' comments can be characterized as falling into the following categories: (a) fighting against perceptions; (b) fighting against institutionalized racism and sexism; and (c) situational advantages. There is more edge to these comments than there was to the superintendents' comments, possibly reflecting the greater attention women in the central office gave to barriers. And for some, the sense of not having made it yet (for the 59% who aspire to the superintendency, for example) prompted them to express their feelings in more outspoken terms.

Fighting against Perceptions

Women of color central office administrators talked about having to prove their worth more often than their white counterparts. Their comments reinforce the sense of being closely scrutinized expressed by the women of color superintendents.

Women of color are continually tested and challenged. We have to work harder—produce more—prove our competency. (1259)

Need to continue to prove one's ability to lead. Some individuals have difficulty dealing with a woman of color. I deal with [those who have difficulty] with great professionalism and feel sorry for their inability to value diversity. (920)

Generally colleagues, supervisors and the general public doubt your competence. I have dealt with this by learning to "toot my own horn," frequently and in many places. (1251)

There are many references to having to work harder and to fight for recognition.

You have to fight for everything. Your decisions are questioned more frequently. Therefore I have kept good documentation to support the majority of my decisions. (1352)

Tried harder, prepared more and learned to speak the "language of power." (1097)

You work harder and smarter and become very astute at knowing political ramifications. (1144)

Several commented on fighting stereotypical beliefs, such as:

The expectation that I am either incompetent or a super-woman who will be tough and aggressive has been part of my experience. I handle this by being true to my belief about how to lead and manage schools. (803)

It is difficult to bring about changes for students of color because people see you as promoting your own race. (1167)

Fighting against Institutionalized Racism and Sexism

The responses of women of color in the central office indicate that discrimination based upon race and sex is a significant perceived problem affecting recognition, promotion, and pay.

My experience has differed from others because I'm frequently placed in areas where there are problems, and expected to "fix" it yet received little recognition for effective changes made during supervision of various programs. My pay differs from others who have done the same work. (621)

Many white male superintendents do not have a doctorate degree but are appointed to those positions. I have a doctorate degree and still cannot be seriously considered because of my race and gender. (863)

Racism is always there and the failure of my board to pay what I feel I am worth. (983)

The power of the white males who have traditionally had a monopoly on educational leadership is clear.

In a southern, rural community where racial biases have existed historically, white males often have difficulty following directives from people of color. (1163)

As a woman of color in a leadership position, it is difficult to gain respect from white old boys administrators. (1167)

Situational Advantages

In contrast to many other responses from either women of color superintendents or women of color in the central office, this group of responses includes comments suggesting that minority status provides an advantage for the participants—either in acquiring needed skills and competencies or in actually gaining a job.

[I'm] sensitive to issues in the community that others may not necessarily see as "issues" (language, modes of communication). (844)

[I'm] more sensitive to the needs of the community—greater empathy with low-income families. (925)

In my state, there are opportunities for women of color—especially Hispanics. (1258)

It is particularly important to capture the sense of efficacy some women of color feel they have as a result of their minority status.

In some ways and in various situations, it has been an advantage to be a woman of color. The good old boys can say they have a minority and are not intimidated by a female so it's easy to make an impact. (481)

People like me. I have decent people skills. I think people feel I'm competent and it's a feather in their cap that they have a black woman as a leader. (771)

On the whole, the many open-ended responses to this question confirmed and expanded the impressions gained from the multiple-choice questions on the survey. Although we were unable to probe the comments for greater meaning, we saw a consistency in the responses that gave us confidence in interpreting them the way we have. What emerges most clearly from these qualitative data is the heightened sense of women of color in leadership positions of being on stage, with their performance continually critiqued. There are no feelings of com-

placency expressed. Instead, feelings of challenge and conflict dominate the responses.

CONCLUSION

Little is known about the lived experiences of superintendents of color
in general and less is known about women superintendents of color.
Likewise, very little is known about women of color in central office
positions. This study makes a major contribution to our knowledge, but
is it still very limited. We urge others to conduct similar studies and to
build on this study to gain deeper and more complex knowledge of
what it is like to be a woman of color educational leader. One final
point must be made very clear. The profile that emerges from this study
shows that the perceptions and beliefs of women leaders of color, and
their experiences of educational administration, differ distinctly from
white women's experiences. In future, we must be careful not to speak
too generally of women's experiences of leadership. Just as men and
women in educational leadership do not share a common set of experiences, neither do white women and women of color. Moreover, it is
very likely that there is still more variety of experiences among women
of different ethnic and linguistic backgrounds than this study has cap-
tured.

Writing of superintendents of color, Juanita Simmons (2005) states
that

> Although today's superintendents of color have needs and problems that
> are common to all superintendents, superintendents of color experience
> additional barriers that are precipitated by race, the economic and social
> deterioration of their minority-populated school districts, and the diffi-
> culty of accessing the necessary political and social power relationships
> (civic capacity building) needed to improve the social and academic per-
> formance of their districts. (p. 271)

This seems a daunting task at best for this population of superintendents, but this study has revealed that women of color are not unduly
deterred by such conditions. More to the point, we read increasingly of

districts making great gains in providing more equitable experiences for students, raising test scores, and reducing drop-out rates (Marshall & Young, 2006). Many of these districts are led by superintendents of color. The determination and tenacity expressed by women of color in this study could well account for such successes.

CHAPTER 7

Conclusion: Flow in the Superintendency

I took the one less traveled by,
And that has made all the difference.

—Robert Frost (1916, p. 9)

Despite being in the glare of the spotlight as superintendent, women must find the job very appealing. On the 2003 survey, 74% of women superintendents described the position as providing considerable self-fulfillment. The question asks, "How much self-fulfillment (that is, the feeling of being able to use one's unique capabilities or realizing one's potential) does your position as superintendent provide" (Question 109, AASA Survey, 2002, p. 18, parentheses in the original). A further 22% describe the superintendency as moderately self-fulfilling. On the 2000 survey, only 56% of the men found the job considerably self-fulfilling.

Mihaly Csikszentmihalyi in his books *Flow* (1990) and *Finding Flow* (1997) gives us several clues as to why women would find the challenges of the superintendency so satisfying. Csikszentmihalyi has long researched what makes a person enjoy his or her work, helping to explain why some people find even tough jobs very satisfying. A number of factors influence a person's ability to find flow or optimal experience in work activities.

The common characteristics of optimal experience are:

a sense that one's skills are adequate to cope with the challenges at hand, in a goal-directed, rule-bound action system that provides clear clues as to how well one is performing. Concentration is so intense that there is no time left over to think about anything irrelevant, or to worry about [personal] problems. Self-consciousness disappears, and the sense of time becomes distorted. An activity that produces such experiences is so gratifying that people are willing to do it for its own sake, with little concern for what they will get out of it, even when it is difficult or dangerous. (1990, p. 71)

The superintendency offers opportunities for the major components of a flow experience. The foremost challenge for the superintendent is to find ways to use human and material resources effectively so that all children in the district learn and develop their potential. Daily challenges are provided with personnel issues, the necessity to comply with ever-increasing numbers of state and federal mandates, student and staff safety concerns, and community politics, to mention a few. In the study, the women participants were asked to rate 30 challenges found in contemporary literature on the superintendency in terms of their significance. Financing schools to meet the increasing current expenditures and capital outlay, and assessing and testing for learner outcomes emerged as the most significant (see Table 7.1). In addition, women were asked to comment on how they would like to see the superintendency changed to make it a more attractive position. In their views, the most challenging aspects of the work included the need for more autonomy, need for more public and professional support, and having to deal with a particularly demanding position.

As reported in chapter 5, some superintendents clearly identified boards of education as a primary obstacle to getting the job done as well as they, as superintendents, would like. Comments ranged from the desire to "Eliminate school boards that are elected . . . the mayor [should] appoint a five person professional management board" (673) to the beliefs that "The superintendency would be more attractive if school board members were better trained and prepared for their roles" (1098) and "It would be easier if local school boards existed in an advisory, not governance capacity. Leading schools is incredibly complex and most lay people have a difficult time understanding all issues" (268).

Meeting the challenge of lay boards certainly emerges as a daily undertaking for women superintendents, but it is not one that derailed women superintendents. For instance, women did not include the challenge "administrator-board relations" as high on their list of most significant challenges—in contrast to their male counterparts. They also

Table 7.1.   Significant Issues Facing the Superintendency Today and Career
Satisfaction

Issue	% Considerable self-fulfillment	% None to moderate self-fulfillment
Financing schools	97	97
Assessing & testing	95	94
Accountability	91	88
Demands for new ways of teaching	90	89
State & federal mandates	87	88
Teacher recruitment/selection	85	76
Changing priorities in curriculum	83	81
Obtaining timely & accurate information for decision making	79	76
Administration/board relations	76	75
Children at risk	70	69
Administrator recruiting	69	68
Strategic planning	69	66
Insufficient funds for technology	69	65
Personal time management	67	69
Collaboration with parents on children's services	63	61
Community involvement	63	58
Changes in societal values	62	68
Parent apathy	59	65
Caliber of school board members	58	64
Changing demographics/effect on race relations, integration, segregation, and immigration	54	56
Caliber of responsibilities of boards of education	48	52

reported a strong and consistent belief in their interpersonal skills as being advantageous to the job. Thus, the key to a satisfying job is to *manage* challenge. "Flow tends to occur when a person's skills are fully involved in overcoming a challenge that is just about manageable" (Csikszentmihalyi, 1997, p. 30).

What do women superintendents do to address these and other challenges? The need for more public and professional support emerged as a major theme in the open-ended comments.

The job should come with a coach or "personal trainer." Not enough money to hire a chief of staff and I am swamped with new issues! (1331)

More support and mentoring—it is difficult to operate in a vacuum, and since you are the only one in this position in a district, it can be very isolating. (1213)

But women superintendents do not sit passively by and bemoan the lack of support. They act.

> I enjoy the superintendency. We have a group of rural superintendents who meets at least twice monthly—it really helps. Such collaborations would assist future candidates in knowing they don't have to go it all alone. (470)
>
> The job will probably never change—we need to prepare better for it. When we survive, we need to help others so they can get a frame of reference for what is "normal." As I learn, I am committed to helping others on their way. (678)

This last comment echoes the enthusiasm women superintendents reported for mentoring others. With only 24% of women superintendents and 37% of women central office administrators reporting having worked for a women superintendent, there are still few role models for aspiring women superintendents. However, 85% of women superintendents and 84% of women central office administrators reported mentoring others aspiring to be a superintendent or administrator. Finding support from others to overcome the isolation of being a woman in a traditionally male occupation seems to be critical for these women. If nothing else, they make use of the state, national, and regional superintendent meetings.

To deal with the need for professional support, women reported keeping up with professional activities offered by educational associations and taking degrees in higher education. Though they are about the same age as their male counterparts, women superintendents are more current in their academic preparation. Forty-seven percent of women superintendents earned their highest degree within the past 10 years, compared to 36% of men. Fifty-eight percent of women superintendents hold doctorates, compared to 44% of men superintendents. In addition, women superintendents manage the current pressure of high-stakes testing and the elimination of the achievement gap by getting professional development in curriculum and instruction. Seventy-three percent of women superintendents participated in opportunities offered by the Association of Supervision and Curriculum Development

(ASCD), compared to 38% of the general population of superintendents (see Table 5.2).

Csikszentmihalyi (1990) explains that flow activities, such as professional development and other opportunities for learning new knowledge and skills, "pus[h] people to higher levels of performance . . . transfor[m] the self by making it more complex" (p. 74). He adds, "In this growth of self lies the key to flow activities" (p. 74). There is strong evidence that women in the superintendency and in the central office pursue multiple avenues to develop the self.

Looking at the career paths of women as they head toward both central office positions and the superintendency, we find that women serve in at least four different positions on their way. And interestingly, over half of those who are women of color have had experience in five or more areas. These positions include teaching and administration. We do not know for sure that every change of position provides opportunities for growth of knowledge and/or skills, but no two situations are exactly alike, so the potential for professional development exists. What seems clear is that women who are interested in higher level administrative positions do not stand still. Only 10% of women superintendents have spent their entire career in one school district.

Once the fork in the yellow wood is taken, women heading toward the superintendency clearly embrace tough challenges along the way to prepare for this demanding role. Perhaps because it is rarely easy going, they become accustomed to meeting challenges instead of avoiding them. Thus, when they reach the position, they develop themselves further as they encounter each new test of their capabilities. Instead of creating burnout conditions, this thorny path appears to provide much satisfaction in the end.

CONSIDERABLE SELF-FULFILLMENT

To understand better what might contribute to the considerable self-fulfillment that nearly three quarters of the women superintendents in the study reported, we cross-tabulated the survey responses of the group who expressed considerable self-fulfillment by the responses of all others. An interesting profile of the highly self-fulfilled women was revealed.

Age seems to be a factor. As might be expected, a higher proportion of those superintendents who are older, who have persevered, and who have not exited the position express considerable self-fulfillment. Self-fulfillment in the position seems to increase with age: 75% of the highly self-fulfilled group were 51 or older.

Raising children also plays a part. Nearly 80% of the highly self-fulfilled women superintendents had raised one or more children. Interestingly, only 30% of those women reported delaying seeking a superintendency until their children were older. That suggests that a good number of women superintendents who are combining the raising of children with the demands of the superintendency are dealing well with those challenges.

There was little to say about the influence of location on self-fulfillment. Three quarters of the population in all districts reported considerable self-fulfillment. The group was fairly evenly distributed among rural districts, small towns, and suburbs. The smallest group was in the large cities, which is representative of the sample as a whole. Worth mentioning of the group in large cities, though, is that 70% reported considerable self-fulfillment—a slightly higher percentage than in any other kind of district.

Related to these findings is the more telling influence of district size. The larger the district women superintendents serve in, the more self-fulfilled they seem to be. Of those in districts of 5,000 students or larger, 80% or more of the women superintendents are highly self-fulfilled. *All* the women superintendents in districts of 50,000 students or larger report considerable self-fulfillment. Two possible factors come to mind to account for the correlation of district size to self-fulfillment. First, in larger districts, superintendents can draw on more personnel to share the duties and responsibilities, and second, larger districts offer greater complexity and less predictable environments. Therefore, on the one hand, superintendents are unlikely to be dealing with routine, mundane matters and, on the other hand, they have more support to deal with crises and political upheaval.

The majority of women superintendents who are highly self-fulfilled followed the career path of teacher, principal, and then central office administrator on the way to the superintendency, although other career paths are represented among this group (see Table 7.2). There is no

Table 7.2. Career Path to the Superintendency and Career Satisfaction

Career path	% Considerable self-fulfillment	% None to moderate self-fulfillment
Teacher/principal/central office	52	47
Teacher/central office	17	17
Teacher/principal	14	23
Other	12	7
Principal/central office	2	1
Teacher only	2	1
Central office only	<1	3
Principal only	<1	<1

particular career path that stands out from the others as potentially providing more self-fulfillment than another. It is clear, however, that spending time in the classroom contributes to the self-fulfillment women express in the superintendency. Sixty-three percent of the highly self-fulfilled women superintendents spent between 6 and 15 years in the classroom.

Similarly, number of years in a superintendency seems to matter (see Table 7.3). Although slightly over half of the group of highly self-fulfilled women superintendents had spent between 1 and 5 years in the position, of those who had spent more than 5 years in the position, 83% expressed considerable self-fulfillment. This is compared to 67% of those who had spent fewer than 5 years in the position. This finding suggests that experience—learning how to deal with the challenges

Table 7.3. Years as a Superintendent and Career Satisfaction

Years	% Considerable self-fulfillment	% None to moderate self-fulfillment
1	10	11
2–3	21	30
4–5	20	30
6–7	13	9
8–9	12	9
10–11	7	6
12–13	7	2
14–15	5	<1
16+	5	2

posed by the superintendency—is a very important factor in finding self-fulfillment in the position.

Moreover, consistent with Csikszentmihalyi's (1990, 1997) notions of optimal experience, women superintendents who accept the different and possibly greater challenges of relocating as superintendent are prominent among the group of highly self-fulfilled women superintendents. Eighty-three percent of those who have held more than one superintendency and 85% of those who have served in more than one state report considerable self-fulfillment.

The act of mentoring seems to be another source of considerable self-fulfillment. Eighty-eight percent of the highly self-fulfilled group were mentoring or had mentored others. Although they are already overloaded with responsibilities, instead of seeing this as a burdensome task, these women superintendents seem to enjoy sharing their skills and insights with others seeking to move into administrative positions like the superintendency.

Interestingly, having a doctoral degree does not seem to be *necessary* for women superintendents to be highly self-fulfilled in the position. Thirty-seven percent of those who are considerably fulfilled do not have a doctoral degree. However, 63% of the women in this group do have a doctorate, and of those who have one, 81% describe themselves as considerably self-fulfilled. So it seems that the higher degree contributes to the feeling of self-fulfillment. In addition, of those who rated their superintendent preparation programs as excellent, 80% are in the highly self-fulfilled group. Thus, academic preparation in degree programs at higher education is associated with the attainment of considerable self-fulfillment. It is likely that the more the degree program helps a woman to prepare for the superintendency, the more satisfying she is likely to find the job. The quality of the degree program is more important to these women than the gaining of a degree.

While women as a whole participated much more than their male counterparts in self-development activities, the highly self-fulfilled group participated in professional development activities slightly more than those who expressed none to moderate self-fulfillment. Consistent across all providers of professional development, the most active participants were superintendents who were highly self-fulfilled. Seventy-four percent of the highly self-fulfilled women superintendents participated in activities offered by both ASCD and AASA, compared to 69% of the moderately or non-self-fulfilled group who participated in AASA and 71% of the moderately or non-self-fulfilled group who participated in ASCD. This level of participation for both groups is considerably higher than in activities offered by other agencies. On a related note, 80% of the highly self-fulfilled group were members of AASA, compared to 75% of the rest of the women superintendents, and 69% of the highly satisfied were members of ASCD, compared to 67% of the others. Membership in organizations and participation in activities seem similarly associated with self-fulfillment.

When considering what skills and knowledge help advance career opportunities for women superintendents or women aspiring to the superintendency, the highly self-fulfilled group believed more strongly than the rest in women's knowledge of teaching and learning (63% compared to 57%) and in the emphasis on improving instruction (65% compared to 61%). When looking at barriers to advancement, as might be expected, the moderately or non-self-fulfilled group was in higher agreement on the importance of most factors than the highly self-fulfilled group with the exception of two factors: lack of mobility for family members (84% of the moderately or non-self-fulfilled group thought it an important or somewhat important factor, compared to 90% of the highly self-fulfilled group), and lack of mentors or mentoring (65% compared to 74%). One possible explanation for the first discrepancy is that slightly more of the highly self-fulfilled group have moved districts in the course of their careers (just over 90% compared to almost 88% of the moderately or non-self-fulfilled group). The experience of relocation could account for the highly self-fulfilled group's placing a stronger emphasis on lack of mobility as a limitation. And regarding mentoring experiences, only 67% of the moderately or non-self-fulfilled superintendents received mentoring, compared to 74% of the highly self-fulfilled. Thus, the value of mentoring is more highly perceived by the latter group than the former, who had attained the position without the benefit of such support.

Of the women superintendents hired to be change agents, 77% are considerably self-fulfilled. Compared to their less fulfilled counterparts, slightly more of the highly self-fulfilled were hired to be change agents (27% versus 24%). When looking at the board's primary expectation of the superintendent, the profile of the considerably self-fulfilled superintendent is a little different from the non-self-fulfilled in a couple of important areas. Slightly more considerably self-fulfilled women were expected to be political leaders (12% compared to 10%), fewer were expected to be managerial leaders (23% compared to 28%), and more were expected to lead reform (11% compared to 7%). Moreover, of those superintendents whose board's primary expectation of them was to lead reform, 83% were considerably self-fulfilled. This fact draws attention to the importance of opportunities for change and the meaning of reform for superintendents.

According to our research, many women superintendents seem to find satisfaction and fulfillment in the engagement of those change and reform activities. These are the opportunities for action Csikszentmiha-lyi (1990) talks about when he makes the point that, for the experience of fulfillment to occur,

> one must learn to balance the opportunities for action with the skills one possesses. . . . many people stagnate because they do not trust their own potential. They choose the safety of trivial goals and arrest the growth of complexity at the lowest level available. (p. 210)

These women superintendents have embraced the challenges of reform and change as providing both the opportunities for action and for the growth of complexity. And, in gaining new knowledge and understanding through their professional development and academic pursuits, they are constantly increasing their capacities to act to achieve the district goals.

Closely related to this is the fact that three quarters of the women superintendents who experienced considerable self-fulfillment received high ratings from their boards. The group of highly self-fulfilled superintendents was significantly more likely to receive an excellent rating from their boards than were their less fulfilled counterparts (75% compared to 56%). In addition, the considerably self-fulfilled group was more than twice as likely as the other group to perceive themselves as very successful (61% compared to 25%). One of the criteria for experiencing flow is that one must be operating in a "rule-bound action system that provides clear clues as to how well one is performing"

(Csikszentmihalyi, 1990, p. 71). Our findings reveal the importance of feedback to help individuals gauge how close they are to achieving their goals (personal and district).

When considering the factors women superintendents believed to be inhibitors to their effectiveness, there was *not* a lot of agreement among them in general. However, the group of highly self-fulfilled superintendents disagreed with the rest on a few noteworthy points. A lot fewer of the former thought board micromanagement to be an inhibitor (17% compared to 29%), and fewer thought there were too many insignificant demands being made on them (36% compared to 41%). At the same time, more of the highly self-fulfilled thought inadequate financing of schools to be an inhibitor. Forty-five percent of the highly self-fulfilled compared to 38% of other superintendents were in agreement on that.

Salary seems to play some role in the self-fulfillment of women superintendents. A majority of the highly self-fulfilled group was earning $100,000 or more, compared to fewer than half of the less fulfilled group (56% compared to 38%; see Table 7.4). Moreover, 83% of superintendents earning $125,000 or more were in the highly fulfilled group, and 100% of those earning $175,000 or more were in the highly self-fulfilled group. In addition, twice as many women superintendents in the highly self-fulfilled group received performance bonuses compared to the other group (14% versus 6%). It seems that a high salary is not a necessary condition for self-fulfillment, but not surprisingly, it is

Table 7.4.   Women Superintendents' Annual Salary

Salary ($)	% Considerable self-fulfillment	% None to moderate self-fulfillment
25,000 or less	<1	0
25,000–50,000	2	2
50,000–75,000	12	17
75,000–100,000	30	43
100,000–125,000	28	22
125,000–150,000	15	12
150,000–175,000	8	3
175,000–200,000	3	0
200,000–225,000	1	0
225,000–250,000	<1	0
250,000+	<1	0

much more likely that those superintendents who are earning a high salary will find the position to be considerably self-fulfilling.

Somewhat contradicting popular beliefs that women superintendents do not necessarily work well with women board members is the fact that 77% of those who report considerable self-fulfillment have two or more women on their boards, compared to 70% of women who report none or moderate self-fulfillment. There is also a striking contrast in the opinions of women superintendents about their board members' qualifications. The highly self-fulfilled group is almost one and a half times more likely to find their board members very well qualified or well qualified (71% compared to 49%). Similarly, the former group is much more likely to describe their boards as active than the latter (75% compared to 58%).

When describing how policy and policy options in their districts are developed, the difference between the considerably fulfilled group and the rest is interesting. Thirty-nine percent of the less fulfilled believe the superintendent develops policy and policy options, but it is the reverse among the considerably self-fulfilled—40% report that the responsibility is shared between the superintendent and the school board chair (see Table 7.5). Moreover, of those who share the responsibility, 80% are considerably self-fulfilled. This finding is quite likely related to the constant feedback necessary to produce a flow experience. In a shared situation, there is much opportunity for interaction between the board president and the superintendent. If this interaction is to be managed well, the superintendent will be receiving many clues as to how well her actions are aligned with the board's goals and objectives.

Table 7.5. Policy Development and Career Satisfaction

Policy development	% Considerable self-fulfillment	% None to moderate self-fulfillment
Shared responsibility	40	29
Superintendent	33	39
School board	11	13
General office staff	11	11
Other	2	4
School board chair	1	3
Principals	<1	1

The considerably self-fulfilled group also engages citizen participation in district decision making more frequently than the less fulfilled group (76% compared to 65%) (see Table 7.7). Similarly, a higher percentage of the highly self-fulfilled group involves parents and citizens in a planning advisory capacity in every area from student activities to program evaluation to objectives and priorities for the school district and strategic planning (see Table 7.8). Consistent with this fact is the finding that the considerably self-fulfilled group gives more weight to all constituents as sources of information for superintendent decision-making. The greatest discrepancy lies in the weight given to teachers and parents. Traditionally, these constituents have not been consulted as often as district administrators, other superintendents, and board members. More than half of the highly self-fulfilled group even gave weight to student input—another long-neglected source (see Table 7.9).

The role stress plays in self-fulfillment is interesting. Csikszentmihalyi (1997) writes of how individuals transform stressful situations into flow experiences.

> One must invest attention into the ordering of tasks, into the analysis of what is required to complete them, into the strategies of solution . . . and while everyone has the psychic energy needed to cope with strain, few learn to use it effectively. (p. 107).

It seems that many of the women superintendents who expressed considerable self-fulfillment have learned how to deal with stress. Only 13% of the considerably self-fulfilled group experienced very great stress in the superintendency compared to 26% of the others (see Table 7.6). Slightly more of the less fulfilled group found considerable stress

Table 7.6. Amount of Stress in the Role of Superintendent

Amount of Stress	% Considerable self-fulfillment	% None to moderate self-fulfillment
No stress	<1	0
Little stress	4	3
Moderate stress	39	24
Considerable stress	44	47
Very great stress	13	26

in the position (47% of the less-fulfilled group compared to 44% of the highly fulfilled group). It appears that some stress is necessary for self-fulfillment because 83% of the highly fulfilled group experienced moderate or considerable stress compared to 71% of the others.

Perceptions of the status and prestige of the superintendency seem also related to self-fulfillment. Eighty percent of those who are considerably self-fulfilled believe that the position of superintendent in their district remained as influential as 10 years ago or was increasing in importance. This is in clear contrast to only 57% of the others. And it is interesting to note that 68% of the highly fulfilled group see themselves continuing in the superintendency until retirement, compared to 54% of the others. Yet another indicator of their satisfaction in the position is that 81% of the considerably self-fulfilled would be superintendents if they had to do it all over again, compared to only 54% of the less self-fulfilled superintendents.

A final set of perceptions sheds some light on which women superintendents find considerable self-fulfillment in the position and which superintendents do not. Differences in the perceptions of the two groups of three percentage points or more appeared in some of their attitudes toward the challenges facing the superintendency. Of those where there was 50% or more agreement among the group's members, the highly self-fulfilled group rated the following challenges as more significant than the latter: accountability/credibility, community involvement in school district decision making, teacher recruitment and selection, obtaining timely and accurate information for decision making, and insufficient funds to purchase and use technology (see Table 7.1). Moreover, the considerably self-fulfilled group was less concerned than the others about these challenges: changing demographics

Table 7.7.   Superintendents Actively Seek Citizen Participation in Decision-Making

Frequency	% Considerable self-fulfillment	% None to moderate self-fulfillment
All the time	15	15
Frequently	61	51
When required	22	29
Seldom	2	5
Never	0	0

and their effect on race relations, integration, segregation, and immigration; caliber of persons assigned to or removed from local boards of education; caliber of responsibilities assigned to or removed from local boards of education; changes in societal values and behavioral norms; and parent apathy and irresponsibility about their own children. The overall picture of these two groups of superintendents is one of contrast. The considerably self-fulfilled group is challenged by technical matters for the most part—issues that they most likely can find strategies to deal with. On the other hand, the less fulfilled group sees challenge in issues over which they have no control or even any impact—such as changing demographics, parent behavior, and the quality of board members.

This contrast points to the possibility that the experience of self-fulfillment, closely related to the experience of flow, is dependent on the autotelic personality of some superintendents—actually, three quarters of the population of women superintendents in the United States at this time.

Csikszentmihalyi (1990) defines the autotelic personality as one that is able to control his or her consciousness:

> For people who have learned to control consciousness focusing attention is relatively effortless, because they can shut off all mental processes but the relevant ones. It is this flexibility of attention . . . that may provide the neurological basis for the autotelic personality. (p. 88)

He writes of individuals who achieve flow as those who are able to recognize opportunities for action in jobs where others do not. They develop skills and learn to focus on the activity at hand so that they value the experience for its own sake. People who find variety in their work, learn to complexify it, create clear goals for which they seek, and are given feedback are more likely to experience enjoyment in their work.

Brunner (2000a) used Castaneda's principles to reflect similar qualities in women superintendents. For instance, Principle 6, Compressing Time, can be likened to the idea that flexible attentiveness is integral to achieving flow. Women superintendents in Brunner's (2000a) study reported the necessity of not wasting a moment of time. Principle 2,

Table 7.8. Superintendent Involves Parents/Citizens in an Advisory Capacity

Areas	% Considerable self-fulfillment	% None to moderate self-fulfillment
Objectives and priorities	68	56
Strategic planning	66	62
Fundraising	65	56
Sch-based decision-making	53	51
Programs/curriculum	53	44
Student activities	44	42
Student behavior	44	40
Finances and budget	39	32
Evaluation of programs	33	25
Other	10	9

Discarding the Unnecessary, expresses the notion that women superintendents learn to focus on the most salient aspects of their work. In her study, Brunner (2000a) reported that they learned to arrange their personal lives so that their lives could support rather than detract from the challenges of their position. And Principle 4, Taking Risks, is consistent with another of the characteristics of an autotelic personality. Csikszentmihalyi (1990) explains that self-centeredness prevents an individual from controlling his or her consciousness: "A self-centered individual . . . evaluates every bit of information only in terms of how it relates to her desires" (p. 84). Risk taking is necessary to free the individual from fear of harming the self so that one can focus on others' needs. Brunner (2000a) found that women superintendents engaged in the kind of risk taking that helped them to abandon their self-consciousness and to enjoy the demands of the position. Flow is achieved in a work situation when an individual takes on the challenges of reaching goals beyond those of self-interest. The superintendency offers many opportunities for such a focus.

Csikszentmihalyi (1990) might have been writing specifically about superintendents when he stated that those in public life are offered especially great opportunities for the optimal experience.

Trying to optimize the goals of unrelated individuals involves complexities an order of magnitude higher [than optimizing one's own goals or those of one's friends and family]. . . . It is much more difficult, but much more fulfilling for the politician to actually improve social conditions, for the philanthropist to help out the destitute. (p. 190).

In other words, if superintendents take up the challenge of helping to maximize the social and academic potential of all students in the district, and of creating a learning community inclusive of teachers, staff, and the wider public, they are likely to find great enjoyment in their work.

The fact that women superintendents find their work to be considerably self-fulfilling suggests that they are developing their potential as leaders. It means that they are not happy with the status quo nor are they dealing passively with challenges and difficulties. It suggests that they have learned to actively seek alternative strategies to the traditional way to do things. If this were not the case, there would not be so many who enjoy the work despite the harsh glare of the media spotlight that could potentially distract them from focusing on the children and their families and cause them to abandon the charge.

CONCLUSION

Robert Frost's poem "The Road Not Taken" has been used in this book as a metaphor for the decision a woman faces in committing to the

Table 7.9.   Significant Weight Given to Sources of Information by Superintendent

Source	% Considerable self-fulfillment	% None to moderate self-fulfillment
School board members	94	89
Principals	92	85
Central office	85	77
Teachers	83	77
Fellow superintendents	76	75
Parents	71	60
Students	51	42
State office staff	48	45
Community groups	43	37
Consultants	39	37
Professional organizations	35	32
Community power structure	34	30
Other	2	2

superintendency. Many of the images suggest that the traveler could just as easily have taken either of the forks in the road. This is very true of the superintendency. In earlier studies and in anecdotes, women superintendents have told us often that they didn't plan on being a superintendent—it just happened. But for some women administrators, there is a strong sense of finding themselves deep in a yellow wood with a choice of roads to take. One leads to places along the path of principal and central office administrator. The other leads to the super-intendency. For women, one more than the other seems particularly risky and unknown. Compared to men, so few women have ever trav-eled along that road.

The narrator in the poem, like many of the central office voices in this study, tells us that she is "sorry [she] could not travel both [roads]/ and be one traveler." Many of the respondents in this study expressed considerable satisfaction with their central office positions. Sixty per-cent of the central office executives did *not* aspire to the superinten-dency. Like the narrator, many women are uncomfortable with the notion of the definitive "fork" in the road that represents a commitment to the superintendency.

Our findings have shown that it is not easy to identify those women who, like the intrepid traveler, decide to take a risk on the untrodden path to the superintendency. They take a chance on that road "as just as fair / And having perhaps the better claim, / Because it was grassy and wanted wear." Nevertheless, our study has confirmed that there are certainly those who are attracted by the idea that "wanting wear" makes a path exciting and worth venturing upon. Moreover, the study confirms that most of those courageous women who traveled down that path to the superintendency feel fulfilled by the "difference" it has made in their lives. They are more than glad they did it. Indeed, by the title, Frost suggests that those who do *not* take "the [road] less trav-eled" are poorer as a result. Those travelers will not experience the satisfaction of being adventurous.

We have considered many factors found in the research to try to explain women administrators' aspirations and motivations. We have been interested in understanding both the decision to aspire to the superintendency and the decision not to pursue the position. In chapter 2, we presented several theories of motivation to help understand what prompts human beings to strive to realize personal and/or professional goals. Theories that relate to job satisfaction and learning as powerful motivators fit well with Csikszentmihalyi's (1990, 1997) work on the flow experience. Because the question of self-fulfillment so clearly differentiated women superintendent's answers from men superintendent's answers, for this population of worker, motivation and aspiration may well be explained by the promise of enjoyment and self-actualization that the superintendency offers.

One of the keys seems to be found in job performance. When rewards and recognition are attached to the level of performance, and when feedback is immediate, the worker finds both clear direction and satisfaction (Csikszentmihalyi, 1990; McCormick & Ilgen, 1980; Lawler & Porter, 1967). Csikszentmihalyi's notion of the autotelic personality is also connected to Beck's (2004) idea that satisfaction and fulfillment in work derives from a sense of control over actions that contribute to success. Clearly, women central office administrators who value high levels of performance and find themselves able to judge wisely the best course of action are likely to be motivated to pursue further opportunities to experience more of the same positive feedback. In addition, women central office administrators with autotelic personalities are likely to seek the greater control over events that the superintendency offers.

The emphasis on learning as a powerful motivator (Blum, 2002; Hall, Lund, & Jackson, 1968; Skinner, 1938) also seems to be very relevant to the findings in this study. The general profile of women superintendents illustrated how highly they valued not only formal academic degrees but also keeping professionally current. Again providing a strong contrast to their male counterparts, women superintendents were found to participate actively in professional development, especially regarding curriculum and instruction. Therefore, women administrators who enjoy furthering their knowledge and skills will be more likely to aspire to a superintendency than those who do not. Interestingly, the enjoyment and challenge of learning appears to be more of a motivator for women to pursue the superintendency than for men, who seem content with the levels of learning they have acquired on the way to the position.

Finally, as Csikszentmihalyi (1990) asserts, self-fulfillment in work is derived from an ability to sustain involvement in the work activity. Individuals who derive satisfaction from the pursuit of their own self-interests will be unable to experience flow. Thus, women administrators who seek greater opportunities to devote themselves to the goals of facilitating the growth and development of all children will be likely to aspire to the position of superintendent. Few women have sought a superintendency for the prestige and status associated with the position. One reason that many women do not seek a superintendency is that many are content with the status and recognition that teaching and other positions in education bring.

But this sense of contentment is less true of women of color. They have a greater sense of urgency and appear to be more highly motivated to reach the top than their white counterparts. Chapter 6 outlined many differences in the profiles of women of color superintendents and white women superintendents. If the road less traveled looks forbidding for white women, it is a treacherous path for women of color in terms of the still prevalent discrimination they face. Yet more women of color appear ready to take the fork toward the superintendency (59% compared to 37%). Moreover, more women of color are actively applying for superintendencies than are white women (40% compared to 28%).

Women of color are often promoted to line positions earlier than their white counterparts, but often without the mentoring and support that is so necessary for success in the position. They often find themselves in administrative positions in the most challenging urban settings. They wait longer for a superintendency than white women do, and they must be even better educated than white women or men. The stakes are higher all round. And it is not surprising that fewer women of color were highly self-fulfilled than white women (67% compared to 75%) or that more women of color superintendents were looking forward to early retirement than white women (14% compared to 7%). On the other hand, more women of color superintendents than white women superintendents would do it over again (82% compared to 73%).

Therefore, although it might be harder for women of color to get where they want to go, they too seem motivated by the opportunities to achieve the goals of better education for all children that the superintendency offers. They have learned that there is more leverage in that position, and, whether by choice or not, they ready themselves for the tough road by acquiring as many experiential and academic qualifications as possible. The image is less one of a traveler who has choices than of a traveler who has a mission to accomplish and who is going to get there whatever it takes.

To be sure, this study illustrates the fact that women are making a name for themselves as superintendents today. Boards of education seek women out for their expertise in instruction, their interpersonal skills, and their community building capacities. And they rate them very highly. Well-educated, highly motivated women will always have opportunities. From what we have learned in this study, we know that more women will lead districts in the future. We are also confident that children and their families will benefit from women's decisions to take that less traveled road.

Appendix: Design of the Study

The American Association of School Administrators (AASA) commissioned this nationwide, descriptive study of women in the superintendency and women assistant/associate/deputy superintendents in order to provide the most up-to-date, comprehensive information on women and the superintendency. Using the AASA membership database and data from Market Data Retrieval, the leading U.S. provider of education mailing lists and databases, 2,500 women superintendents were identified and surveys were mailed to them. In addition, 3,000 surveys were sent to women holding central office positions of assistant superintendent or higher. Eventually, 723 superintendents and 472 central office personnel responded. Nearly 30% of the total population of women superintendents is thus represented in this national sample. Market Data Retrieval listed 13,728 districts in 2000. This research indicates that approximately 18% of districts are led by women—the highest national figure recorded.

The survey used for the study included around 100 short-response questions and eight open-ended questions. In addition to other questions, the survey asked: What are your experiences? Does the superintendency appeal to you? What changes would you like to see? How do you lead? What are your issues? Since there is no single model of a woman superintendent or central office administrator, the aim of the study was to gather all the stories and profiles from women of color, from those with nontraditional backgrounds, from younger leaders and more mature ones, and from those serving in urban, rural, and suburban settings.

References

Abramson, L. Y., Seligman, M. E., & Teasdale, J. (1978). Learned helplessness in humans: Critique and reformulation. *Journal of Abnormal Psychology, 87,* 49–74.

Adler, A. (1917). *Neurotic constitution.* New York: Moffat & Ward.

Ah Nee-Benham, M. (2003). In our mother's voice: A native woman's knowing of leadership. In M. D. Young & L. Skrla (Eds.), *Reconsidering feminist research in educational leadership* (pp. 223–245). Albany: State University of New York Press.

Ah Nee-Benham, M., & Cooper, J. (1998). *Let my spirit soar! Narratives of diverse women in leadership.* Thousand Oaks, CA: Corwin Press.

Allport, G. W. (1960). *Personality and social encounter.* Boston, MA: Beacon.

Alston, J. A. (1999). Climbing hills and mountains: Black females making it to the superintendency. In C. C. Brunner (Ed.), *Sacred dreams: Women and the superintendency* (pp. 79–90). Albany: State University of New York Press.

Alston, J. A. (2000). Missing from action: Where are the black female school superintendents? *Urban Education, 35*(5), 525–531.

Alston, Judy A. (2005). Tempered radicals and servant leaders: Black females persevering in the superintendency. *Educational Administration Quarterly, 41*(4), 675–688.

Amsel, A. (1992). *Frustration theory.* New York: Cambridge University Press.

Anthony, R., Roe, J., & Young, M. D. (2000). *Selecting new administrators for tomorrow's administration.* Iowa City, IA: Educational Placement Consortium.

Atkinson, J. W. (1958). *Motives in fantasy, action, and society.* New York: D. Van Nostrand.

Banks, C. M. (1995). Gender and race as factors in educational leadership and administration. In J. A. Banks & C. A. McGee Banks (Eds.), *Handbook of research on multicultural education.* New York: Macmillan.

Barlow, D. H. (2000). Unraveling the mysteries of anxiety and its disorders from the perspective of emotion theory. *American Psychologist, 55,* 1245–1263.

Beck, R. C. (2004). *Motivation: Theories and principles* (5th ed.). Upper Saddle River, NJ: Prentice Hall.

Beekley, C. (1999). Dancing in red shoes: Why women leave the superintendency. In C. C. Brunner (Ed.), *Sacred dreams: Women and the superintendency* (pp. 161–176). Albany: State University of New York Press.

Bell, C. (1988). Organizational influences on women's experience in the superintendency. *Peabody Journal of Education, 65*(4), 31–59.

Bell, C. (1995). "If I weren't involved with schools, I might be radical": Gender consciousness in context. In D. Dunlap & P. Schmuck (Eds.), *Women leading in education* (pp. 288–312). Albany: State University of New York Press.

Bell, C., & Chase, S. (1993). The underrepresentation of women in school leadership. In C. Marshall (Ed.), *The new politics of race and gender* (pp. 141–154). London: Falmer.

Bell, C., & Chase, S. (1995). Gender in the theory and practice of education leadership. *Journal for a Just and Caring Education, (1)* 2, 200–23.

Bell, C., & Chase, S. (1996). The gendered character of women superintendents' professional relationships. In K. Arnold, K. Noble, & R. Subotnick (Eds.), *Remarkable women: Perspectives on female talent development* (pp. 117–131). Cresskill, NJ: Hampton.

Bell, P. A., Fisher, J. D., & Loomis, R. J. (1978). *Environmental psychology.* Philadelphia: W. B. Saunders.

Berlyne, D. E. (1960). *Conflict, arousal, and curiosity.* New York: McGraw-Hill.

Biklen, S., & Brannigan, M. (1980). *Women and educational leadership.* Lexington, MA: Lexington Books.

Björk, L. G., Bell, R., & Gurley, K. (2002). Politics and the socialization of superintendents. In G. Perreault (Ed.), *The changing world of educational administration* (pp. 294–331). Lanham, MD: Scarecrow Press.

Blount, J. M. (1998). *Destined to rule the schools: Women and the superintendency, 1873–1995.* Albany: State University of New York Press.

Blount, J. M. (1999). Manliness and the gendered construction of school administration in the USA. *International Journal of Leadership in Education: Theory and Practice, 2*(2), 55–68.

Blum, D. (2002). *Love at Goon Park: Harry Harlow and the science of affection.* Cambridge, MA: Perseus.

Bower, G. H., McLean, J., & Meacham, J. (1966). Value of knowing when reinforcement is due. *Journal of Comparative and Physiological Psychology, 62,* 183–192.

Brown, J. S. (1961). *The motivation of behavior.* New York: McGraw-Hill.

Brunner, C. C. (1997). Working through the "riddle of the heart": Perspectives from women superintendents. *Journal of School Leadership, 7*(2), 138–164.

Brunner, C. C. (1998a). The new superintendency supports innovation: Collaborative decision making. *Contemporary Education, 69*(2), 79–82.

Brunner, C. C. (1998b). Can power support an "ethic of care"? An examination of the professional practices of women superintendents. *Journal for a Just and Caring Education, 4*(2), 142–175.

Brunner, C. C. (1999a). *Sacred dreams: Women and the superintendency.* Albany: State University of New York Press.

Brunner, C. C. (1999b). Taking risks: A requirement of the new superintendency. *Journal of School Leadership, 9*(4), 290–310.

Brunner, C. C. (2000a). *Principles of power: Women superintendents and the riddle of the heart.* Albany: State University of New York Press.

Brunner, C. C. (2000b). Unsettled moments in settled discourse: Women superintendents' experiences of inequality. *Educational Administration Quarterly, 36*(1), 76–116.

Brunner, C. C. (2002a). A proposition for the reconception of the superintendency: Reconsidering traditional and nontraditional discourse. *Educational Administration Quarterly, 38*(3), 402–431.

Brunner, C. C. (2002b). Bane or benefit? Considering the usefulness of research focused on women superintendents. In B. Cooper & L. Fuscerilla (Eds.), *The prom-ise and perils facing today's school superintendent* (pp. 221–246). Lanham, MD: Scarecrow Press.

Brunner, C. C. (2003). Invisible, limited, and emerging discourse: Research practices that restrict and/or increase access for women and people of color to the superinten-dency. *Journal of School Leadership, 13,* 428–450.

Brunner, C. C. (2005). Women performing the superintendency: Problematizing the normative alignment of conceptions of power and constructions of gender. In J. Col-lard & C. Reynolds (Eds.), *Leadership, gender and culture: Male and female per-spectives* (pp. 121–135). Two Penn Plaza, NY: Open University Press.

Brunner, C. C., Grogan, M., & Björk, L. (2002). Shifts in the discourse defining the superintendency: Historical and current foundations of the position. In J. Murphy (Ed.), *The educational leadership challenge: Redefining leadership for the 21st cen-tury, part one* (pp. 211–238). Chicago: University of Chicago Press.

Brunner, C. C., Grogan, M., & Prince, C. (2003, April). *AASA national survey of women in the superintendency and central office: Preliminary results.* Paper pre-sented at the annual conference of the American Educational Research Association, Chicago, IL.

Brunner, C. C., & Peyton-Caire, L. (2000). Seeking representation: Supporting Black female graduate students who aspire to the superintendency. *Urban Education, 35*(5), 532–548.

Brunner, C. C., & Schumaker, P. (1998). Power and gender in the "new view" public schools. *Policy Studies Journal, 26*(1), 30–45.

Byrk, A. S., & Schneider, B. (2002). *Trust in schools: A core resource for improve-ment.* New York: Russell Sage Foundation.

Butts, R. F., & Cremin, L. A. (1953). *A history of education in American culture.* New York: Henry Holt.

Cannon, W. B. (1927). The James-Lange theory of emotions: A critical examination and an alternative theory. *American Journal of Psychology, 39,* 106–124.

Cavalier, R. (2000). *Personal motivation: A model for decision-making.* Westport, CT: Praeger.

Chase, S. E. (1995). *Ambiguous empowerment: The work narratives of women school superintendents.* Amherst: University of Massachusetts Press.

Chase, S. E., & Bell, C. S. (1990). Ideology, discourse, and gender: How gatekeepers talk about women school superintendents. *Social Problems, 37*(2), 163–177.

Cohen, S., & Weinstein, N. (1981). Nonauditory effects of noise on behavior and health. *Journal of Social Issues, 37,* 36–70.

Cooper, B. S., Fusarelli, L. D., & Carella, V. A. (2000). *Career crises in the school superintendency? The results of a national survey.* Arlington, VA: American Asso-ciation of School Administrators.

Coyne, J. C., & Gotlib, I. H. (1983). The role of cognition in depression: A critical appraisal. *Psychological Bulletin, 94,* 472–505.

Csikszentmihalyi, M. (1990). *Flow: The psychology of optimal experience.* New York: HarperCollins.

Csikszentmihalyi, M. (1997). *Finding flow: The psychology of engagement with every-day life.* New York: Basic Books.

Cunningham, L., & Hentges, J. (1982). *The American school superintendency 1982: A summary report.* Arlington, VA: American Association of School Administrators

Darley, A. (1976). Big-time careers for the little woman: A dual-role dilemma. *Journal of Social Issues, 32*(3), 85–97.

Deci, E. L. (1975). *Intrinsic motivation.* New York: Plenum Press.

Deci, E. L., & Ryan, R. M. (1985). *Intrinsic motivation and self-determination in human behavior.* New York: Plenum Press.

Dillard, C. (1995). Leading with her life: An African-American feminist for an urban high school principal. *Educational Administration Quarterly, 31*(4), 539–563.

Dillard, C. (in press). *On spiritual strivings: Transforming an African American woman's academic life.* Albany: State University of New York Press.

Dollard, J., & Miler, N. E. (1941). *Social learning and imitation.* New Haven, CT: Yale University Press.

Dreikurs, R. (1969). Social interest: The basis of normalcy. *Counseling Psychologist, 1,* 45–48.

Duffy, E. (1934). Emotion: An example of the need for reorientation in psychology. *Psychological Review, 41,* 184–198.

Edson, S. (1988). *Pushing the limits: The female administrative aspirant.* Albany: State University of New York Press.

Eisenberger, R., & Rhoades, L. (2001). Incremental effects of reward on creativity. *Journal of Personality and Social Psychology, 81,* 728–741.

Enomoto, E. K., Gardiner, M. E., & Grogan, M. (2000). Notes to Athene: Mentoring relationships for women of color. *Urban Education, 35*(5), 567–583.

Estler, S. E. (1975). Women as leaders in public education. *Signs: Journal of Women in Culture and Society, 1*(2), 363–386.

Eysenck, M. J., (1997). *Anxiety and cognition: A unified theory.* East Sussex, England: Psychology Press.

Frost, R. (1916). *Mountain interval.* New York: Henry Holt and Company.

Funk, S. C., & Houston, B. K. (1987). A critical analysis of the Hardiness Scale's validity and utility. *Journal of Personality and Social Psychology, 53,* 572–578.

Gaertner, K. N. (1980). The structure of organizational careers. *Sociology of Education, 54*(1), 7–20.

Gardiner, M. E., Enomoto, E., & Grogan, M. (2000). *Coloring outside the lines: Mentoring women into school leadership.* Albany: State University of New York Press.

Glass, T. (1992). *The study of the American school superintendency 1992: America's education leaders in a time of reform.* Arlington, VA: American Association of School Administrators.

Glass, T. & Björk, L. G. (2003). The superintendent shortage: Findings from research on school board residents. *Journal of School Leadership, 13*(3), 265–287.

Glass, T. E., Björk, L., & Brunner, C. C. (2000). *The study of the American school superintendency, 2000: A look at the superintendent of education in the new millennium.* Arlington, VA: American Association of School Administrators.

Grady, M., Ourada-Sieb, T., & Wesson, L. (1994). Women's perceptions of the superintendency. *Journal of School Leadership, 4*(2), 156–170.

Gray, J. (1982). *The psychology of fear and stress.* New York: McGraw-Hill.

Gribskov, M. (1980). Feminism and the woman school administrator. In D. K.

Biklen & M. B. Brannigan (Eds.), *Women and educational leadership* (pp. 77–91). Lexington, MA: D. C. Heath.

Grogan, M. (1996). *Voices of women aspiring to the superintendency.* Albany: State University of New York Press.

Grogan, M. (1999). Equity/equality issues of gender, race, and class. *Educational Administration Quarterly, 35*(4), 518–536.

Grogan, M. (2000). A Black woman superintendent tells. *Urban Education, 35*(5), 597–602.

Grogan, M., & Brunner, C. C. (2005a, February). Women leading systems. *School Administrator, 62*(2), 46–50.

Grogan, M., & Brunner, C. C. (2005b). Women superintendents and role conception: (Un)troubling the norms. In L. G. Björk & T. J. Kowalski (Eds.), *The contemporary superintendent: Preparation, practice, and development* (pp. 227–250). Thousand Oaks, CA: Corwin Press.

Grogan, M., & Henry, M. (1995). Women candidates for the superintendency: Board perspectives. In B. Irby & G. Brown (Eds.), *Women as school executives: Voices and visions* (pp. 146–173). Huntsville, TX: Texas Council for Women School Executives.

Hackman, J. R., & Lawler, E. E. (1971). Employee reactions to job characteristics. *Journal of Applied Psychology, 55,* 259–286.

Hackman, J. R., & Oldman, G. R. (1976). Motivation through the design of work: Test of the theory. *Organizational Behavior and Human Performance, 16,* 250–279.

Hall, J. (1961). *The psychology of motivation.* Philadelphia: J. P. Lippincott.

Hall, R. V., Lund, D., & Jackson, D. (1968). Effects of teacher attention on study behavior. *Journal of Applied Behavior Analysis, 1,* 1–12.

Hammen, C. L. (1985). Predicting depression: A cognitive-behavior perspective. In P. C. Kendall (Ed.), *Advances in cognitive-behavioral research and therapy* (Vol. 4, pp. 30–71). New York: Academic Press.

Hansot, E., & Tyack, D. (1981). *The dream deferred: A golden age for women school administrators* (Policy Paper No. 81-C2). Palo Alto, CA: Stanford University Institute for Research on Educational Finance and Governance.

Harlow, H. F. (1953). Mice, monkeys, men, and motives. *Psychological Review, 60,* 23–32.

Hebb, D. O. (1955). Drives and the CNS (conceptual nervous system). *Psychological Review, 62,* 243–254.

Hecker, M. H., Chesney, M. A., Black, G. W., & Frautschi, N. (1988). Coronary-prone behaviors in the Western Collaborative Group Study. *Psychosomatic Medicine, 50,* 153–164.

Heider, F. (1958). *The psychology of interpersonal relations.* New York: Wiley.

Helgesen, S. (1990). *The female advantage: Women's ways of leadership.* New York: Doubleday.

Hennig, M., & Jardim, A. (1977). *The managerial woman.* New York: Anchor Press.

Henry, A. (2000). Thoughts on black women in the workplace: Space not intended for us. *Urban Education, 35*(5), 520–524.

Herzberg, F. (1966). *Work and the nature of man.* New York: New American Library.

Hodgkinson, H., & Montenegro, X. (1999). *The U.S. school superintendent: The invisible CEO.* Washington, DC: Institute for Educational Leadership.

Holmes, T. H., & Rahe, R. H. (1967). The social readjustment rating scale. *Journal of Psychosomatic Research, 11,* 213–218.

Houston, P. (1998). The ABCs of administrative shortages. *Education Week, 17*(38), 32–44.

Hull, C. L. (1943). *Principles of behavior.* New York: Appleton-Century-Crofts.

Jackson, B. L. (1995). *Balancing act: The political role of the urban school superintendent.* Washington, DC: Joint Center for Political and Economic Studies.

Jackson, B. L. (1999). Getting inside history—against all odds: African-American women school superintendents. In C. C. Brunner (Ed.), *Sacred dreams: Women and the superintendency* (pp. 141–160). Albany: State University of New York.

Johnsrud, L. K. (1991). Administrative promotion: the power of gender. *Journal of Higher Education, 62*(2), 119–149.

Jones, E., & Montenegro, X. (1983). Factors predication women's upward career mobility in school administration. *Journal of Educational Equity and Leadership, 3*(3), 231–241.

Kalbus, J. C. (2000). Path to the superintendency. *Urban Education, 35*(5), 549–556.

Kamler, E., & Shakeshaft, C. (1999). The role of search consultants in the career paths of women superintendents. In C. C. Brunner (Ed.), *Sacred dreams: Women and the superintendency* (pp. 51–62). Albany: State University of New York Press.

Kobasa, S. C. (1979). Stressful life events, personality and health: An inquiry into hardiness. *Journal of Personality and Social Psychology, 37,* 1–11.

Kowalski, T. (2003). *Contemporary school administration* (2nd ed.). Boston: Allyn & Bacon.

Kowalski, T., & Brunner, C. C. (2005). The school district superintendent. In F. English (Ed.), *The handbook of educational leadership* (pp. 142–167). Thousand Oaks, CA: Corwin Press.

Lawler, E. E., & Porter, L. W. (1967). The effects of performance on job satisfaction. *Industrial Relations, 20,* 20–28.

Lazarus, R. S. (1981). Little hassles can be dangerous to your health. *Psychology Today, 15,* 58–61.

Lepper, M., & Greene, D. (1978). *The hidden cost of reward.* New York: Lawrence Erlbaum.

Levine, S. (1960). Stimulation in infancy. *Scientific American, 202,* 80–86.

Lewin, K. (1935). *A dynamic theory of personality.* New York: McGraw-Hill.

Lewin, K., Dembo, T., Festinger, L., & Sears, P. S. (1944). Level of aspiration. In J. McV. Hunt (Ed.), *Personality and the behavior disorders* (pp. 333–378). New York: Ronald Press.

Lindsley, D. B. (1951). Emotion. In S. S. Stevens (Ed.), *Handbook of experimental psychology.* New York: Wiley.

MacLeod, J. (1987). *Ain't no makin it: Leveled aspirations in a low-income neighborhood.* Boulder, CO: Westview Press.

Maienza, J. G. (1986). The superintendency: Characteristics of access for men and women. *Educational Administration Quarterly, 22*(4), 59–79.

Marshall, C. (1985). The stigmatized woman: The professional woman in a male sextyped career. *Journal of Educational Administration, 13*(2), 131–152.

Marshall, C., & Young, M. D. (2006). The wider societal challenge: An afterword. In

C. Marshall & M. Oliva (Eds.), *Leadership for social justice: Making revolutions in education* (pp. 307–315). Boston, MA: Pearson Education.

Maslow, A. H. (1970). *Motivation and personality,* (2nd ed.). New York: Harper & Row. (Original work published 1948)

McAdams, D. P. (1997). A conceptual history of personality psychology. In R. Hogan, J. Johnson, & S. Briggs (Eds.), *Handbook of personality psychology* (pp. 4–27). New York: Academic Press.

McClelland, D. C. (1958). Risk-taking in children with high and low need for achievement. In J. W. Atkinson (Ed.), *Motives in fantasy, action, and society* (pp. 306–378). Princeton, NJ: Van Nostrand.

McClelland, D. C. (1971). *Assessing human motivation.* Morristown, NJ: General Learning Press.

McClelland, D. C. (1975). *Power: The inner experience.* New York: Irvington.

McClelland, D. C. (1985). *Human motivation.* New York: Cambridge University Press.

McCormick, E. J., & Ilgen, D. R. (1980). *Industrial psychology* (7th ed.). Englewood Cliffs, NJ: Prentice-Hall.

McDougall, W. (1923). *Outline of psychology.* New York: McGraw-Hill. (Original work published 1908)

Méndez-Morse, S. E. (1999). Re-definition of self: Mexican American women becoming superintendents. In C. C. Brunner (Ed.), *Sacred dreams: Women and the superintendency* (pp. 125–140). Albany: State University of New York Press.

Méndez-Morse, S. E. (2000). Claiming forgotten leadership. *Urban Education, 35*(5), 584–595.

Méndez-Morse, S. E. (2003). Chicana feminism and educational leadership. In M. D. Young & L. Skrla (Eds.), *Reconsidering feminist research in educational leadership* (pp. 161–178). Albany: State University of New York Press.

Méndez-Morse, S. E. (2004). Constructing mentors: Latina educational leaders' role models and mentors. *Educational Administration Quarterly, 39,* 561–590.

Miller, N. E. (1951). Learnable drives and rewards, In S. S. Stevens (Ed.), *Handbook of experimental psychology* (pp. 435–472). New York: Wiley.

Miller, N. E. (1959). Liberalization of basic S-R concepts: Extensions to conflict behavior, motivation and social learning. In S. Koch (Ed.), *Psychology: A study of a science* (Vol. 2). New York: McGraw-Hill.

Montenegro, X. (1993). *Women and racial minority representation in school administration.* Arlington, VA: American Association of School Administrators.

Morris, W. (Ed.). (1981). *American Heritage dictionary of the English language.* Boston, MA: Houghton Mifflin.

Mountford, M. (2001). *An exploration of motivations for school board membership, conceptions of power, and their effects on decision making.* Unpublished doctoral dissertation, University of Wisconsin, Madison.

Mountford, M. (2004). Motives and power of school board members: Implications for school board-superintendent relationships. *Educational Administration Quarterly, 40*(5), 704–741.

Murray, H. A. (1938). *Explorations in personality.* New York: Oxford University Press.

Murtadha-Watts, K. (2000). Cleaning up and maintenance in the wake of an urban school administration tempest. *Urban Education, 35*(5), 603–615.

Nogay, K., & Beebe, R. J. (1997). Gender and perceptions: Females as secondary principals. *Journal of School Leadership, 7,* 246–265.

Nozaki, Y. (2000). Feminist theory and the media representation of a woman-of-color superintendent: Is the world ready for *Cyborgs? Urban Education, 35*(5), 616–629.

Ortiz, F. I. (1982). *Career patterns in education: Women, men and minorities in public school administration.* New York: Praeger.

Ortiz, F. I. (1991). An Hispanic female superintendent's leadership and school district culture. In N. Wyner (Ed.), *Current perspectives on the culture of school* (pp. 29–43). Cambridge, MA: Brookline Books.

Ortiz, F. I. (1999). Seeking and selecting Hispanic female superintendents. *Sacred dreams: Women and the superintendency* (pp. 91–102). Albany: State University of New York.

Ortiz, F. I. (2000). Who controls succession in the superintendency: A minority perspective. *Urban Education, 35*(5), 557–566.

Ortiz, F. I. (2001). Hispanic females' school leadership: Cases of superintending. In C. C. Brunner & L. G. Björk (Eds.), *The new superintendency* (pp. 87–94). New York: JAI Press.

Ortiz, F. I., & Marshall, C. (1988). Women in educational administration. In N. Boyan (Ed.), *Handbook of research on educational administration* (pp. 123–141). New York: Longman.

Ortiz, F. I., & Ortiz, D. J. (1995). How gender and ethnicity interact in the practice of educational administration: The case of Hispanic female superintendents. In R. Donmoyer, M. Imber, & J. Scheurich (Eds.), *The knowledge base in educational administration: Multiple perspectives* (pp. 158–173). Albany: State University of New York Press.

Pavan, B. N. (1999). The first years: What should a female superintendent know beforehand? In C. C. Brunner (Ed.), *Sacred dreams: Women and the superintendency* (pp. 105–124). Albany: State University of New York Press.

Pitner, N. (1981). Hormones and harems: Are the activities of superintending different for a woman? In P. Schmuck, W. Charters, & R. Carlson (Eds.), *Educational policy and management: Sex differentials* (pp. 273–295). New York: Academic Press.

Reid, R. L. (Ed.). (1982). *Battleground: The autobiography of Margaret A. Haley.* Urbana: University of Illinois Press.

Reith, J. (1988). Job satisfaction parallels in higher education. Unpublished master's thesis, Wake Forest University, Winston-Salem, NC.

Rescorla, R. A., & Solomon, R. L. (1967). Two-process learning theory: Relationships between Pavlovian conditioning and instrumental learning. *Psychological Review, 74,* 151–182.

Revere, A. B. (1986). *A description of black female school superintendents.* Unpublished doctoral dissertation, Miami University of Ohio.

Rogers, C. R. (1942). *Counseling and psychotherapy.* New York: Houghton Mifflin.

Rolls, E. T. (1999). *The brain and emotion.* New York: Oxford University Press.

Rosener, J. B. (1990). Ways women lead. *Harvard Business Review, 68*(6), 119–125.

Rothbaum, F., Weisz, J. R., & Snyder, S. S. (1982). Changing the world and changing the self: A two-process model of perceived control. *Journal of Personality and Social Psychology, 42,* 5–37.

Sadker, M., Sadker, D., & Klein, S. (1991). The issue of gender in elementary and sceondary education. *Review of research in education* (pp. 269–334). Washington, DC: American Educational Research Association.

Sanders-Lawson, R., Smith-Campbell, S., & Benham, M. K. P. (2006). Wholistic visioning for social justice: Black women theorizing practice. In C. Marshall & M. Oliva (Eds.), *Leadership for social justice* (pp. 31–63). Boston: Pearson Education Inc.

Sansone, C., & Harackiewicz, J. M. (Eds.). (2000). *Intrinsic and extrinsic motivation.* New York: Academic Press.

Scherr, M. W. (1995). The glass ceiling reconsidered: Views from below. In P. M. Dunlap & P. A. Schmuck (Eds.), *Women leading education* (pp. 313–323). Albany: State University of New York Press.

Schmuck, P. (1975). *Sex differentiation in public school administration.* Arlington, VA: American Association of School Administrators.

Schmuck, P. (1980). Changing women's representation in school management. In S. Biklen & M. Brannigan (Eds.), *Women in educational leadership* (pp. 239–259). Lexington, MA: Lexington Books.

Schmuck, P. (1982). *Sex equity in educational leadership: The Oregon story.* University of Oregon-Eugene: Center for Educational Policy and Management.

Schmuck, P. A., Charters, W. W., & Carlson, R. O. (1981). *Educational policy and management: Sex differentials.* San Diego, CA: Academic Press.

Seligman, M. E., Abramson, L. Y., Semmel, A., & von Bayer, C. (1979). Depressive attributional style. *Journal of Abnormal Psychology, 88,* 242–247.

Sexton, P. (1976). *Women in education.* Indiana: Phi Delta Kappa.

Shakeshaft, C. (1989). *Women in educational administration* (3rd ed.). Newbury Park, CA: Corwin Press.

Shakeshaft, C. (1999). The struggle to create a more gender-inclusive profession. In J. Murphy & K. Seashore-Louis (Eds.), *Handbook of research on educational administration,* (2nd ed., pp. 99–118). San Francisco: Jossey-Bass.

Shakeshaft, C., Gilligan, A., & Pierce, D. (1984, April). *Does dissertation research have anything to do with scholarship?* Paper presented at the annual meeting of the American Educational Research Association, New Orleans.

Sherman, D., & Repa, T. (1994). Women at the top: The experiences of two superintendents. *Equity and Choice, 10*(2), 59–64.

Simms, M. (2000). Impressions of leadership through a Native woman's eyes. *Urban Education, 35*(5), 637–644.

Simmons, J. C. (2005). Superintendents of color. In L. Björk and T. Kowalski (Eds.), *The contemporary superintendent* (pp. 251–281). Thousand Oaks, CA: Corwin Press.

Skinner, B. F. (1938). *The behavior of organisms.* New York: Appleton-Century-Crofts.

Skinner, B. F. (1953). *Science and human behavior.* New York: Macmillan.

Skrla, L. (1999, April). *Femininity/masculinity: Hegemonic normalizations in the public school superintendency.* Paper presented at the annual meeting of the American Educational Research Association, Montreal, Canada.

Sklra, L. (2000a). Mourning silence: Women superintendents (and a researcher) rethink speaking up and speaking out. *International Journal of Qualitative Studies in Education, 13*(6), 611–628.

Skrla, L. (2000b). The social construction of gender in the superintendency. *Journal of Education Policy, 15*(3), 293–316.

Skrla, L., & Benestante, J. J. (1998). On being terminally female: Denial of sexism in educational administration is no protection against its effects. In C. Funk, A. Pankake, & M. Reese (Eds.), *Women as school executives: Realizing the vision* (pp. 57–61). Commerce: Texas A&M University Press.

Skrla, L., Reyes, P., & Scheurich, J. J. (2000). Sexism, silence, and solutions: women superintendents speak up and speak out. *Educational Administration Quarterly, 36*(1), 44–75.

Smith, F. J. (1977). Work attitudes as predictors of attendance on a specific day. *Journal of Applied Psychology, 62,* 16–19.

Staw, B. M. (1976). *Intrinsic and extrinsic motivation.* Morristown, NJ: General Learning Press.

Stewart, A. J. (1982). *Motivation and society.* San Francisco: Jossey-Bass.

Strober, M., & Tyack, D. (1980). Why do women teach and men manage? *Signs, 5*(3), 494–503.

Tallerico, M. (1999). Women and the superintendency: What do we really know? In C. C. Brunner (Ed.), *Sacred dreams: Women and the superintendency* (pp 29–48). Albany: State University of New York Press.

Tallerico, M. (2000a). *Accessing the superintendency: The unwritten rules.* Thousand Oaks, CA: Corwin Press & the American Association of School Administrators.

Tallerico, M. (2000b). Gaining access to the superintendency: Headhunting, gender, and color. *Educational Administration Quarterly, 36*(1), 18–43.

Tallerico, M. (2003). Policy, structural, and school board influences on superintendent supply and demand. *Journal of School Leadership, 13*(3), 347–364.

Tallerico, M., & Blount, J. (2004). Women and the superintendency: Insights from theory and history. *Educational Administration Quarterly, 40*(5), 633–662.

Tallerico, M., & Burstyn, J. N. (1996). Retaining women in the superintendency: The location matters. *Educational Administration Quarterly, 32,* 642–664.

Tallerico, M., Burstyn, J. N., & Poole, W. (1993). *Gender and politics at work: Why women exit the superintendency.* Fairfax, VA: National Policy Board for Educational Administration.

Taylor, S. E. (1989). *Positive illusions: Creative self-deception and the healthy mind.* New York: Basic Books.

Thorndike, E. L. (1913). *The psychology of learning.* New York: Teachers College.

Truett, C. (1979, March 18–21). *Women in educational administration: Is there a basic role conflict?* Paper presented at a conference on women and work, in Bloomington, Indiana. (ERIC Document Reproduction Service No. ED172440)

Tyack, D., & Hansot, E. (1982) *Managers of virtue: Public school leadership in America, 1820–1980.* New York: Basic Books.

Tyack, D., & Hansot, E. (1990). Learning together: A history of coeducation in American schools. New Haven, CT: Yale University Press.

U.S. Census Bureau (2000). Census 2000 special EEO (Equal Employment Opportunity) tabulation. *http://www.oesc.state.ok.us/LMI/publications/AffirmAction/2005/eeoTabulation.pdf.*

Waller, W. (1932). *The sociology of teaching.* New York: John Wiley.

Weiner, B. (1985). *Human motivation.* New York: Springer-Verlag.

Wesson, L. H., & Grady, M. (1995). A leadership perspective from women superintendents. In B. J. Irby & G. Brown (Eds.), *Women as school executives: Voices and visions* (pp. 35–41). Huntsville, TX: Sam Houston Press.

Wheatley, M. (1981). The impact of organizational structures on issues of sex equity. In P. A. Schmuck, W. W. Charters, Jr., & R. O. Carlson (Eds.), *Educational policy and management: Sex differentials.* New York: Academic Press.

Wiggins, T., & Coggins, C. (1986). Gender bias in superintendent selection: A projective analysis. *Journal of Educational Research, 80,* 115–120.

Williams, J. J. G., Watts, F. N., McLeod, C., & Mathews, A. (1997). *Cognitive psychology and emotional disorders* (2nd ed.). Chichester, U.K.: Wiley.

Woodworth, R. S., & Schlosberg, H. (1954). *Experimental psychology* (Rev. ed.). New York: Holt, Rinehart & Winston.

Young, I. P. (1984). An examination of job satisfaction for female and male public school superintendents. *Planning and Changing, 15,* 114–124.

Young, M. D., & McLeod, S. (2001, October). Flukes, opportunities, and planned interventions: Factors affecting women's decisions to become school administrators. *Educational Administration Quarterly, 37*(4), 462–502.

About the Authors

C. Cryss Brunner, Ph.D. is an associate professor in the Department of Educational Policy and Administration at the University of Minnesota and joint director of the UCEA Center for the Study of the Superintendency. Her research on women, power, the superintendency, the gap between public schools and their communities, technology and leadership preparation, and constructions of identity has appeared in multiple chapters and such journals as *Educational Administration Quarterly, Educational Policy, Journal for a Just and Caring Education, The Journal of Educational Administration, Policy Studies Journal, The School Administrator, Educational Considerations, Urban Education, Contemporary Education, On the Horizon,* and the *Journal of School Leadership.* In addition to authoring, *Principles of Power: Women Superintendents and the Riddle of the Heart* (2000), she has edited one book, *Sacred Dreams: Women and the Superintendency* (1999), and co-edited another with Lars Björk, *The New Superintendency* (2001). She is one of the co-authors of the *American Association of School Administrators' Ten-Year Study of the School Superintendency* (2000).

Brunner is the 1996–97 recipient of the National Academy of Education's Spencer Fellowship for her work on the relationship between superintendents' conceptions of power and decision-making processes. She is the 1998 recipient of the University Council for Educational Administration's Jack Culbertson Award for her outstanding contributions to the field as a junior professor. Along with Margaret Grogan, Brunner was recognized in 2006 by the American Association of School Administrators (AASA) for 10 years of research on women in the superintendency. She has received numerous fellowships, such as the University of Minnesota's Multi-cultural Teaching and Learning Lifetime Fellowship, and grants related to her identity-sensitizing technology process, *Experiential Simulations (ES),* which prepares leaders to work in multicultural and diverse settings.

Margaret Grogan is currently professor and chair, Department of Educational Leadership and Policy Analysis, University of Missouri—Columbia. She was the 2003–2004 President of the University Council for Educational Administration. Originally from Australia, she received a Bachelor of Arts degree in Ancient History and Japanese Language from the University of Queensland. She taught in a public high school in Australia before moving to Japan. She was a teacher and an administrator at an international school in Tokyo, where she lived for 17 years. During that time, she received her Master of Arts degree in Curriculum and Instruction from Michigan State University. After graduating from Washington State University with a Ph.D. in Educational Administration, she taught in Principal and Superintendent Preparation Programs at the University of Virginia for 8 years. She has published many articles and chapters and has authored, co-authored, or edited four books, including *Women Leading School Systems.* Her current research focuses on women in leadership, the superintendency, the moral and ethical dimensions of leadership, and leadership for social justice. She also edits a series on Women in Leadership for SUNY Press.